I0040840

Pathways to Positioning:

Success Language

Work-Life Skills That Position You for Success

Facilitator: _____   Date: _____

P.O. Box 588, Olney, MD 20830-0588 • Web: www.SpringboardTraining.com

Pathways to Positioning: Success Language
Work-Life Skills That Position You for Success

Program Reference Manual

V-Twin Press
P.O. Box 588
Olney, MD 20830-0588
301-260-1538

Find us online at www.V-TwinPress.com
To report errors, please visit www.SpringboardTraining.com – "Contact Us"

V-Twin Press is a division of Springboard Training, LLC.

© Springboard Training | Sylvia Henderson

ISBN 13: 978-1-932197-40-2
ISBN 10:   1-932197-40-0

"Every life has a story."
- *A&E Biography*

This reference material is a valued resource for

_____

[Name]

Please return to:

_____

[Contact Information]

" I don't have to try and be somebody when I already am."
- *Burt K. League*

Program Description

Your workplace atmosphere, style of communication, expectations, rules, symbols, norms–written and unwritten— constitute a workplace "language" that when understood and communicated, influence the success of individual workers, managers…and customers. This language of success rewards those who learn it and discourages those who do not. An individual learns this success language to position oneself to be hired, considered for advancement and promotion to greater responsibility and status, or to gain new clients.

Those who influence your success are to understand what you say and write, accept how you look and behave, and approve of your work ethic and accomplishments. You must cause them to recognize your knowledge and skills and respond to your attitudes and behaviors before you can advance to more-challenging responsibilities and higher-performing positions and opportunities. (Also, before you can effect changes that grow your career, build your business, or improve your life situation.)

This **"Pathways to Positioning: Success Language"** program teaches (and reinforces) the work-life skills that contribute to your positioning for workplace, professional, and life success. You will use this comprehensive workbook to personalize and internalize your learning experiences. Active participatory exercises inspire your individual self-assessments and group discussions that lead to specific solutions for improving your professional skills and attitudes. Facilitator lectures and additional reading materials provide the information, resources, and guidance that direct you to the knowledge you need to implement the skills and attitudes cultivated throughout the program. Principles of adult learning guide the development and implementation of this program to maximize learner retention.

---

10 Key "Portable Skills" for Life Success

"Portable skills" are skills that, once acquired, you use in every phase of your life – professionally and personally – to succeed where you seek to succeed. These are also skills that you never stop learning, practicing, and improving throughout your life.

- Writing.
- Speaking; communication.
- Teamwork; working with other people.
- Solving problems; making decisions.
- Initiative.
- Cool under pressure.
- Attention to detail.
- Time management.
- Honesty.
- Love of learning (formal and informal).

Source: CollegeBoard.com

Add one more skill— which is more of a personal trait—to this list:
- Having a positive work ethic.

Learning Objectives

By the end of this program, participants (you) will be able to:

- Describe three powerful elements that determine your success;
- Identify four pathways to positioning for your job, career, volunteer, and/or life success;
- Determine the aspects of appearance, communication, behavior, and results that best apply to you and your professional and personal life situations;
- Apply attitudes and implement behaviors that influence how others perceive you and your organization;
- Recognize how you affect others by what you say and do (and vice versa); and
- Make decisions about the influences in your professional and personal life to determine the levels of success you achieve;

using tools provided in the program and engaging the resources you have in each other.

This page intentionally blank.

Program Resource Manual: Table of Contents
(Page numbers prefaced by "P2P-SL" → *Pathways to Positioning: Success Language Program)*

"This book is a wealth of knowledge."
"Keep the quotations; they are inspiring."
"I like how you provide references for further study."
"The reading material is in short doses for easy consumption."
- *Unsolicited comments from workshop participants*

This page intentionally blank

Introductions / Networking

Greatest achievement.

_____

Most prized possession or valued experience.

_____

Favorite T-shirt / bumper sticker / quotation.

_____

Most fun ever had / best trip ever taken.

_____

Be anything you could be.

_____

Stranded – two books.

• _____
• _____

Two people you most like to meet.

• _____
• _____

Name:	Name:
Title:	Title:
Organization:	Organization:
Address:	Address:
Phone – Voice:	Phone – Voice:
Phone – Cell:	Phone – Cell:
Social Network:	Social Network:
E-mail:	E-mail:
Web site:	Web site:
Notes:	Notes:

> "You are the person who has to decide
> Whether you do it or toss it aside.
> You are the person who makes up your mind
> Whether you lead or linger behind;
> Whether you reach for the goal that is far,
> Or just be contented to stay where you are."
> - *Edgar A. Guest*

This page intentionally blank

Success Formula: Three Powerful Elements That Determine Your Success

> # Perception + Performance = Position

Fill in the blank for the following statement as it pertains to you:

"I want / aspire to _____."

It matters not to what area of your life you refer. You can note a professional goal; personal desire; business objective; or other "want." Most of us interact with other people in order to achieve our goals or acquire what we seek. How our interactions unfold directly affects whether we succeed in our endeavors.

Key points:

- **Perception**
  - How people perceive you to be (whether true about you or not.)
  - Has a direct correlation to how people perceive your organization (brand; image.)
- **Performance**
  - What you do and what you achieve.
  - Either proves (supports) or disproves people's perceptions of you.
- **Position**
  - The position to which you aspire.
  - Financial, career, business, political, spiritual, or otherwise.
  - Position = personal power.

One without the other leaves your positioning in question.

- *Ex:* If people perceive you to have solid leadership potential (perception), yet you perform poorly with your current responsibilities, then your positioning as a candidate for promotion to a leadership role in your organization is endangered.
- *Ex:* If you follow the steps you think you should follow to initiate a relationship—personal or professional (performance), yet people perceive you to be rude or socially unpleasant (to them), then your positioning to build that relationship is weak.

Continually ask yourself...

↝ "How can I move from...?"

| ACCEPTABLE |
⇩
| GOOD |
⇩
| EXCELLENT |

↝ "How can I grow from...?"

| EMPLOYEE |
⇩
| LEADER |

Perception = Perspective

Behaviors Representing "Professionalism"

P	
R	
O	Organized
F	
E	
S	Solution-oriented
S	
I	
O	
N	
A	
L	

Additional Resource: Appendix

- "Professionalism—Self Assessment," p.67.
- "I Wish I Had That In School," p.76.

Employment Listing #1

"Professionalism - Approaches others in a tactful manner; Reacts well under pressure; Treats others with respect and consideration regardless of their status or position; Accepts responsibility for own actions; Follows through on commitments."

Employment Listing #2

"Strong sense of professionalism; ability to focus efforts and energy on successfully attaining clear, concrete, accurate timely and measurable outcomes of importance to the customer."

Many more similarly noted!

Ten Steps Towards Success

1. Use language well. Enunciate words clearly and correctly.
2. Associate with people who are where you want to be. Help others who want to earn a place beside you. Encourage those who want to work at moving beyond you. There is room for all.
3. Be pleasant around other people.
4. Learn to compete, and win fairly.
5. Know and appreciate from where you come. Release yourself from the bonds that hold you. Get on board with strategies that propel you forward.
6. Remove excuses, negative language, name-calling, and labeling from your vocabulary and thoughts.
7. Be noticed for your positives.
8. Accept that ten minutes early is "on time."
9. Adopt and maintain a strong work ethic – one that reflects the environment you want.
10. Take the initiative. Be responsible. Make your own researched choices for your life.

‒ *S. Henderson.*
"Success Language" cards.

Pathways to Positioning: Overview

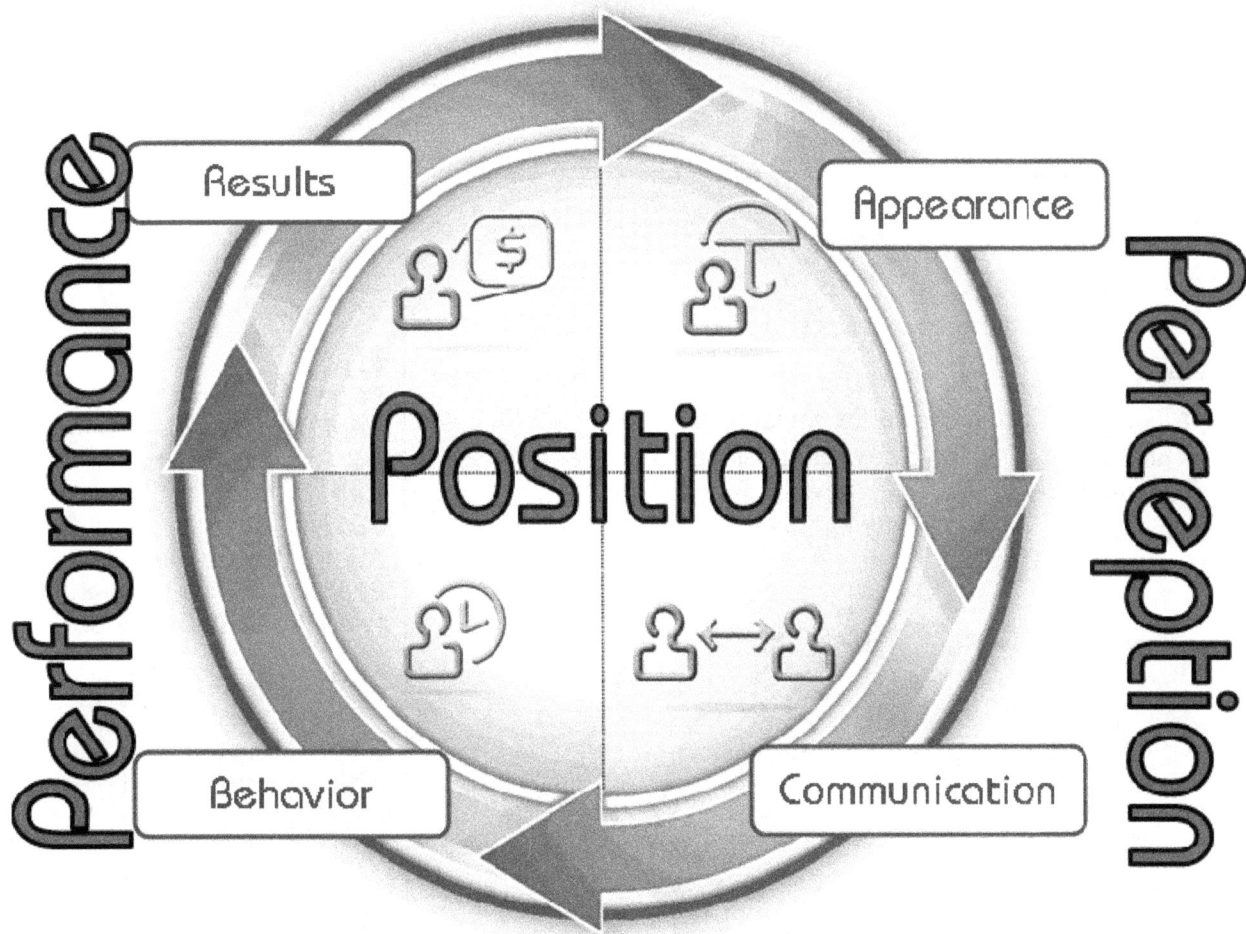

© www.SpringboardTraining.com

Your Four Pathways to Positioning

- Appearance
- Communication ⎫ Perception
- Behavior
- Results ⎫ Performance

Key points:

- Each pathway interacts with the others for total positioning for success (in your job; profession; business; life.)
- "Total package" is most important.
- Missing one or more pathways, while being skilled at others, detracts from positioning.

Reference Scenarios: Appendix

- "Pathways Scenarios: Set 1," p.72.
- "Pathways Scenarios: 'Success Language' Cards," p.73.

Refer to a scenario and answer these questions:

1. Which pathway is / pathways are missing?
2. How might this affect overall positioning?
3. What do you suggest as a solution?

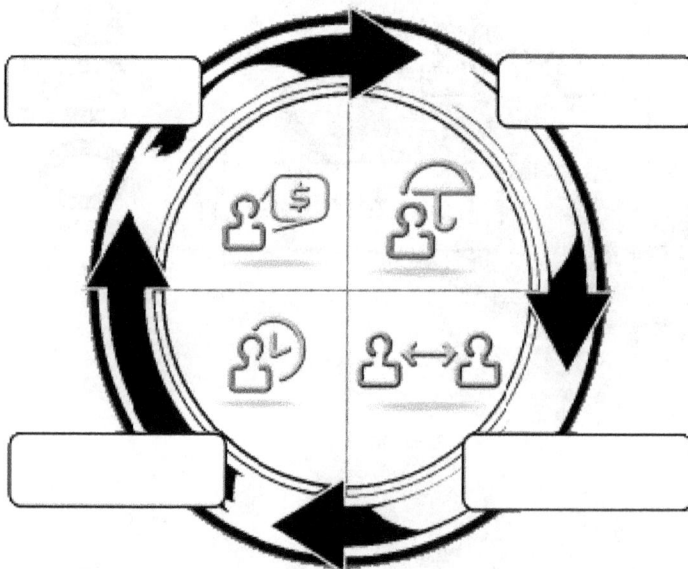

> "You have brains in your head. You have feet in your shoes. You can steer yourself any direction you choose."
> – Dr. Seuss

"Success Language" Resources / Job Aids

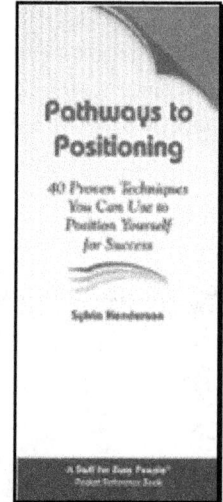

Pathways to Positioning
40 Proven Techniques You Can Use to Position Yourself for Success
Sylvia Henderson

(1)
Pocket Reference Book: *Pathways to Positioning – 40 Proven Techniques You Can Use to Position Yourself for Success*.
Author: Sylvia Henderson.
Publisher: V-Twin Press.
ISBN #1-932197-26-5.

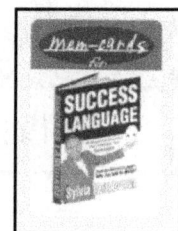

Mem-cards SUCCESS LANGUAGE

(2)
"*Success Language*" card deck.
Author: Sylvia Henderson.
Publisher: Mem-Cards™.
ISBN #1-932197-04-4.

Both are available at http://www.springboardtraining.com/products

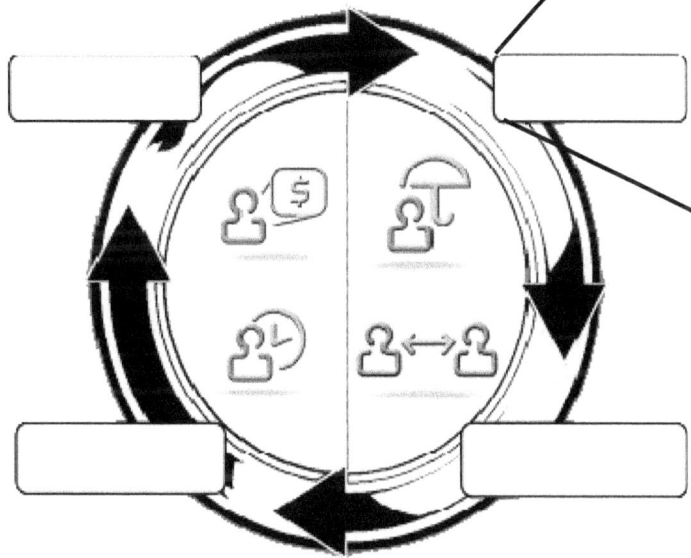

Pathway #1 : Appearance

This page intentionally blank

Pathway #1: Appearance

Elements of appearance:

- Physical
- Emotional
- Attitudinal

> "Every choice you make has an end result."
> - *Zig Ziglar*

A. Physical

Grooming and Attire—The "Look of Success"

"Success" looks to me like…	What I need to do:

First Impressions

You make your own choices as to how others initially react to you. Examine your choices objectively and honestly regarding what you wear and how you look. Do not get angry with people when they respond to you a certain way. Realize that first impressions are based solely on how you present yourself to others. Evaluate your appearance and other people's initial reactions to you. Decide for yourself if you will change or live with the results.

*Source: **Success Language** Card Deck, by Sylvia Henderson.
Card #23. Publisher: Mem-Cards™. ISBN # 1932197044.*

When "Bling" Is Your Thing—Artifacts

The "stuff" you wear and carry with you—accessories, jewelry, and other accoutrements that complement (or detract from) what you wear and how you look—is referred to in urban culture as bling. In the study of interpersonal communication, these objects are known as artifacts. Artifacts are inanimate objects with which you associate that convey a message about you. As you work towards success in your life, beware of the bling—the "stuff" of success. Make sure that your accessories send the message that you want to send.

*Source: **Success Language** Card Deck. Card #24.*

Notes

> "Early impressions are hard to eradicate from the mind."
> - *Unknown*

Judgment—Your Chance, Your Choice

When I wear...	I look / feel like...	Others see / perceive...	Reactions include...

> "Reality is merely an illusion, albeit a very persistent one."
> – *Albert Einstein*

Additional Resources: Appendix
"Dress for Success" (Bibliography), p.69.

Additional Reading: Appendix
Additional "Guidelines for Attire," p.69.

Your organization's employee handbook should have dress code expectations.

Business Attire and Grooming Guidelines

Look successful as you move towards success. Quality garments wear longer, fit better, and save you money in the long run. If your clothing projects a professional image, people tend to respond to you in kind. These suggestions help you present a professional image.

Everyone

- Keep your hair and nails clean and neat.
- Wear appropriate jewelry. Remove excess accessories to avoid distractions.
- Avoid overpowering, "heavy" fragrances.
- Use cosmetics in moderation.
- Shine your shoes.
- Wear neat, clean, pressed, comfortable clothing appropriate to your audience and occasion.

Men

- Wear a suit jacket when you conduct business outside your office. Your authority travels with you.
- Avoid wearing short-sleeved shirts under suit coats.
- Show clean shirt cuffs.
- Avoid ankle socks or light-colored socks with a dark suit.

Women

- Wear comfortable shoes and hosiery to complement your outfit.
- Wear natural looking makeup.
- Avoid elaborate hairstyles.
- Avoid wearing jeans, revealing clothing, and trendy fashions with built-in obsolescence.

To net it out → avoid extremes; **eliminate distractions.**

Attitude—Personal Presence and Confident Comportment

B. Emotional

Stress

> "In the midst of movement and chaos, keep stillness inside of you."
> *- Deepak Chopra*

Stress is a condition or feeling experienced when a person perceives that demands exceed the personal and social resources the individual is able to mobilize. People feel little stress when they have the time, experience and resources to manage a situation. They feel great stress when they think they cannot handle the demands put upon them. Therefore, stress is typically a negative experience. It is not an inevitable consequence of an event: It depends a lot on people's perceptions of a situation and their real ability to cope with it.

Experiencing stress can seldom be compartmentalized. Stressful personal situations may affect a person's health and transcend to the professional environment to affect performance. "Check your problems at the door" is easier said than done. An external intervention may be appropriate in order to work through the stressful situation.

Some people find that certain levels of stress motivate them to action and greater productivity. However, the physical manifestation of stress-induced ailments over time counter the productivity achieved and the underlying causes should still be addressed.

Stress Props

Props are what you use or do to which you transfer your stressful feelings (cigarettes; addictions; unhealthy relationships; pencil-tapping; excessive laughing; others).

What are yours?

📄 **Additional Resource: Appendix**

"Make Mellow Mental Moments" (A Relaxation Exercise), p.70.

Stress Reaction Journal

- What causes stress reactions for you?
- What happens to you (physically) when you feel stress?
- How is your performance affected when you feel stressed over a short period of time? Long period of time?
- What do you do about lessening stressful situations?
- How do you de-stress yourself physically? Mentally? Emotionally?
- What roles do faith / beliefs / values play in helping you manage stress?
- How can you improve (reduce negative levels of) your stress reactions?

Work Environment

↗ Other people.
↗ Constant change.
↗ "The Economy."
↗ Life happens.
} Typical work environment; typical issues.

> "If you choose not to decide, you have made a choice."
> *- Neil Peart*

Is yours any different? Are your issues any different?

↷ We want a positive work environment, yet what does this mean to you and for you?
↷ How do you classify your own work environment?
↷ How does your work environment affect your emotions?
↷ How does your work environment, therefore, affect how you appear to others?

Now—<u>who sets the stage</u> for a positive work environment?
↷ If you answered anyone else other than yourself, what can YOU do to create a positive work environment?

Remember that **the only person you can really change is you**.
(More on this, later, RE: the "Attitude—Behavior—Reaction Loop" on p.24.)

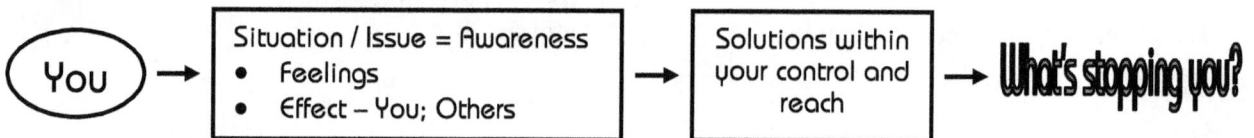

You → | Situation / Issue = Awareness • Feelings • Effect – You; Others | → | Solutions within your control and reach | → **What's stopping you?**

My work environment feels positive when…

One area I would like to improve within my work environment is…

☐
↷ List your ideas for how this can happen. ☐
↷ Put a checkmark next to the suggestions / ☐
solutions that YOU can initiate or implement. ☐
☐

Pick one check-marked solution. Make your plan for making it happen.
↷ Whom do you need to help you?
↷ Whose support?
↷ What resources?

What can you do, yourself, if no one else will help?

📄 Additional Reading: Appendix
- "Positive Work Environment: You Work the Controls," p.90.
- "The Travelers and the Monk," p.93.

Who Is Your Social Support Network?

Identify your social support network.

Name the person...	Whom you can...
	Trust with your secrets.
	Talk with about money issues of concern to you.
	Laugh with.
	Go to for help no matter the problem.
	Pick up your conversation where you left off, whether you last spoke to them yesterday or a year ago.
	Cry on their shoulder (literally).
	Talk with about "old times."
	Share your wildest dreams.
	Talk with about family problems.
	Depend on to motivate you; provide a positive outlook.
	Count on, even if they have their own primary relationship with someone else.
	Give your honest feedback to who will take you seriously and consider your opinions.
	Look up to with respect and admiration.
	Serve as a role model to and guide in their life.

Additional Reading and Resources: Appendix
- "Solid Social Support Networks," p.97.
- Resources for Personal and Emotional Issues, p.98.

> "The greatest happiness of life is the conviction that we are loved; loved for ourselves, or rather, loved in spite of ourselves."
> – *Victor Hugo*

Humor—A Funny Thing About Humor and the Brain

Researchers using advanced imaging techniques continually learn about how the brain processes humor. Observing images of chemical changes in the brain leads to the thought that humor gives people a "natural high" by activating the same reward centers in the brain that are linked to happiness and drug-induced euphoria.

In a study published in *Neuron* magazine, researchers used magnetic resonance imaging (MRI) to study how the brains of 16 healthy adults responded to funny vs. non-funny cartoons. The brain scans detected areas of the brain that were activated when the subject found the cartoon funny. The study showed that in addition to activating areas of the brain involved in language processing, humor also stimulated regions of the brain known as reward centers, such as the amygdala, which releases dopamine. Dopamine is a powerful chemical that plays a vital role in the brain's pleasure and reward system.

Source: WebMD Health News

Dig deep! Identify something you find humorous about…

- Does identifying a humorous situation—even when unintended—cause you to view the situation differently?
- How?
- What can you do for yourself to keep a humor perspective for the next time you need a chuckle?

📄 Additional Reading: Appendix

- "Is It Work When There's Humor?" p.86.
- "Humor—Lightness @ Work and In Life" (Self-Assessment), p.74.

> "Laugh and the world laughs with you. Weep and you weep alone."
> - *Late Nineteenth Century Proverb, from Wilcox*

Your commute

Your workplace

A memo / e-mail / note you read

Your children or pets

A recent doctor's or dentist's visit

A question you were asked

A comment made in a meeting

A tough situation, made lighter

Yourself

Life!

C. Attitudinal

Mindset

> "Watch your thoughts, for they become words.
> Watch your words, for they become actions.
> Watch your actions, for they become habits.
> Watch your habits, for they become character.
> Watch your character, for it becomes your destiny."
> - *Unknown. Source: "Character" Quotations at ThinkExist.com*

	+	-
The media to which I am exposed is mostly…		
The words I use are typically…		
The people with whom I spend at least 8 hours/day project energy that is usually…		
At the end of my non-work activities I feel…		
My primary relationships are…		
My thoughts about myself are, overall…		

For a positive mindset:

- Change your vocabulary. Eliminate words like "can't," "won't" and "failure." The language you use influences the way you think.
- "Throw the boomerang." Perform one unselfish service each day. Your actions—positive or negative—eventually come back to you. "Little things mean a lot."
- Avoid chronic complainers and other negative people as much as possible. "Misery loves company."
- Change the subject to a positive one. Be the one people describe as "always cheerful."
- Stay informed of what is happening in the world, yet understand how media works. Usually, only "bad news" is news. Counter balance each negative with at least five pieces of positive information.
- Convert "should-a; could-a; would-a" to "shall, can, and will."
- Make a list of the traits, habits, attitudes and skills that will exemplify the ideal you, then make every effort to follow those guidelines.

mind·set or mind-set *n.*

1. a fixed mental attitude or disposition that predetermines a person's responses to and interpretations of situations.
2. an inclination or a habit.

The American Heritage® Dictionary of the English Language, Fourth Edition Copyright © 2009 by Houghton Mifflin Company.

In decision theory… a set of assumptions, methods or notations held by one or more people or groups of people that is so established it creates a powerful incentive within these people or groups to continue to adopt or accept prior behaviors, choices, or tools.

- Mental inertia
- Groupthink
- Paradigm

It is typically difficult to counteract the effects upon analysis and decision-making processes. On the positive side, a mindset can also be seen as incident of a person's philosophy of life.

> "Garbage in; garbage out."
> – *Computer programming adage (Note: Works for the human mind, also.)*

Attitude ➲ Behavior ➲ Reaction Loop

Notes

Additional Resource: Appendix

"Pathways Scenarios, Set 2," p.95.

Additional Readings: Appendix

- "More Attitude / Behavior Theory: The Betari Box," p.75.
- "In Position for the Curves—Initiate <u>Your</u> Attitude Change," p.92.

↷ What about "their" behaviors affects your attitude?
↷ Your reaction?
↷ How do you influence "their" behavior?
↷ What can (or do) you do to positively influence how "they" react to you?

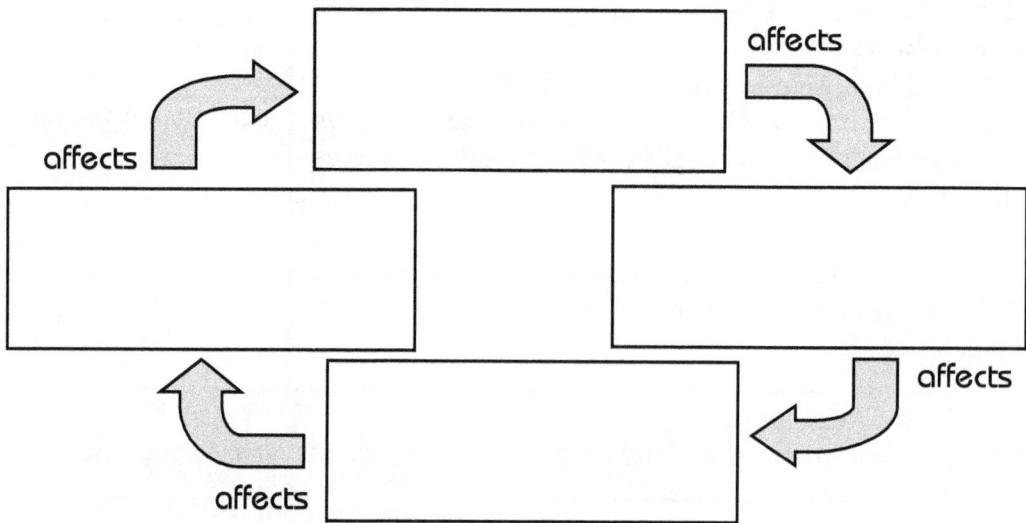

"One hundred percent of the shots you don't take don't go in."
– *Wayne Gretzky, NHL Hockey Player*

Writing Affirmations

> "Our subconscious minds have no sense of humor, play no jokes and cannot tell the difference between reality and an imagined thought or image. What we continually think about eventually will manifest in our lives."
> – Sidney Madwed

Affirmations are simple statements that we make about our decisions in life. We make statements about ourselves to ourselves constantly—sometimes consciously; sometimes automatically. When we make the same statements frequently enough they become subconscious messages.

Our belief system is stored in our subconscious mind. The subconscious mind is like a computer. It takes input, processes it, and produces output. The adage "garbage in; garbage out" is appropo to our subconscious mind.

When we input negative messages, our output is negative attitudes and behaviors. Conversely when we provide positive input we have positive outcomes. This happens over time, through repetition.

Consequently our affirmations are to be positive statements, simply stated, repeated regularly and over time.

Other points about affirmations:

- **Use the present tense** ("I am"; "I choose to be") rather than future tense ("I will'; "I want to be.")
- **Make statements positive** ("I choose to dismiss gossip" rather than "I do not gossip.")
- Written statements are good; **written and spoken statements are better**. More of your senses are involved in making the statements multiplying the input to your subconscious mind.
- **Be specific and make goals attainable.** ("I make $100,000.00 a year" rather than "I am rich.")

Affirmations

- I say these affirmations to myself EVERY DAY.
- I read these affirmations out loud DAILY.
- I do at least one thing every day to support these affirmations.
- I truly believe and envision that which I have written here. IT IS TO HAPPEN FOR ME!

My Affirmations

[Your signature here]

Resources for Affirmations: Appendix
"Positive Attitudes / Authentic Living," p.75.

Practice Makes Perfect

> "It's the repetition of affirmations that leads to belief. And once that belief becomes a deep conviction, things begin to happen."
> – *Claude M. Bristol*

Format A

6	4	1
3	7	9
8	2	5

Period	Time
1	_____
2	_____
3	_____
4	_____
5	_____

Format B

8	10	4	15
14	3	11	5
12	16	7	2
1	6	13	9

Period	Time
1	_____
2	_____
3	_____
4	_____
5	_____

> "One comes to believe whatever one repeats to oneself sufficiently often, whether the statement be true of false. It comes to be dominating thought in one's mind."
> – *Robert Collier*

Past, Present, and Future: Change Happens

Learn from your past; own your present; proactively shape your future.

Change is Certain and Constant
(Are You Ready to Embrace It?)

> "Change is the only constant."
> - *Heraclitus, Greek Philosopher*

A few "change" statistics:

- Every two or three years, the knowledge base doubles.
- Every day, 7000 scientific and technical articles are published.
- Satellites orbiting the globe send enough data to fill 19 million volumes in the Library of Congress—every two weeks.
- High school graduates are exposed to more information than grandparents were in a lifetime.
- A diminishing percentage of jobs will require a college education, yet nearly all jobs will require the equivalent knowledge and analytical skills of a college education.
- There will be as much change in the next three decades as there was in the last three centuries.

Source: "Leadership and Technology." Published by the National School Boards Association—Institute for the Transfer of Technology to Education.

Manage Personal and Professional Change

- Identify what is within your control to change.
- Identify your options.
  - Are you worse off if you make a change, or if you do not?
- Create a support system.
  - Build and maintain relationships with people who are your social support network.
  - Work with colleagues to cope with change together.
- Examine your attitude.
  - Accept that change will happen—with you or without you.
  - Will you live life accepting or rejecting change?
- Remain flexible.
  - Remember "Murphy's Law."
- Give yourself a break.
  - Lighten up and accept that everything is not easy.
- Strive to achieve balance and perspective.

Additional Reading and Resource: Appendix

- "What Is 'Murphy's Law?'" p.79.
- Life Events Change Assessment, p.77.

Change Happens!

Know your own pace for change. Admit how quickly or slowly you handle the pace of change. Avoid setting yourself up for failure.

Your change pace depends on:

- *Safety*: Your need to feel secure before trying something new.
- *Specificity*: Your need to start with small steps and be specific.
- *Age*: Your ability to make and adapt to changes as you age. (Increase in age decreases pace of adaptability.)
- *Time*: The time you need to allow yourself to break old habits.
- *Attitude*: The level of your believe that you cannot change. (Belief becomes your self-fulfilled prophecy=reality.)

Search: YouTube.com for the most-current version of the video, "Did You Know? Shift Happens"

> "The ultimate measure of a [man] is not where [he] stands in moments of comfort and convenience, but where [he] stands at times of challenge and controversy."
> - *Dr. Martin Luther King, Jr.*

Got Change?

Within the past year (12 months) the changes I / we encountered include:	
Personal	*Professional / Job / Career-Related*

↻ Did the changes surprise you? Why?

↻ How prepared were you for the changes?

↻ How did you <u>feel</u>?

↻ How did you <u>react</u>?

↻ How did you help yourself get through the changes?

↻ How did you help others as their change agent? Leader?

↻ How did you facilitate the process for / within your organization?

↻ What will you do differently the next time you encounter similar change?

A Responsible Body

"There was a most important job
That needed to be done,
And no reason not to do it,
There was absolutely none.
But in vital matters such as this,
The thing you have to ask
Is who exactly will it be
Who'll carry out the task?"

"**Anybody** could have told you
That **everybody** knew
That this was something **somebody**
Would surely have to do.
Nobody was unwilling;
Anybody had the ability.
But nobody believed
That it was their responsibility."

"It seemed to be a job
That anybody could have done,
If anybody thought he was
Supposed to be the one.
But since everybody recognized
That anybody could,
Everybody took for granted
That somebody would."

"But nobody told anybody
That we are aware of,
That he would be in charge
Of seeing it was taken care of.
And nobody took it on
Himself to follow through,
And do what everybody thought
That somebody would do."

"When what everybody needed, so,
Did not get done at all,
Everybody was complaining that
Somebody dropped the ball.
Anybody then could see it was
An awful crying shame,
And everybody looked around
For somebody to blame."

"Somebody should have done the job
And Everybody should have,
But in the end Nobody did
What Anybody could have."

– Charles Osgood, Journalist

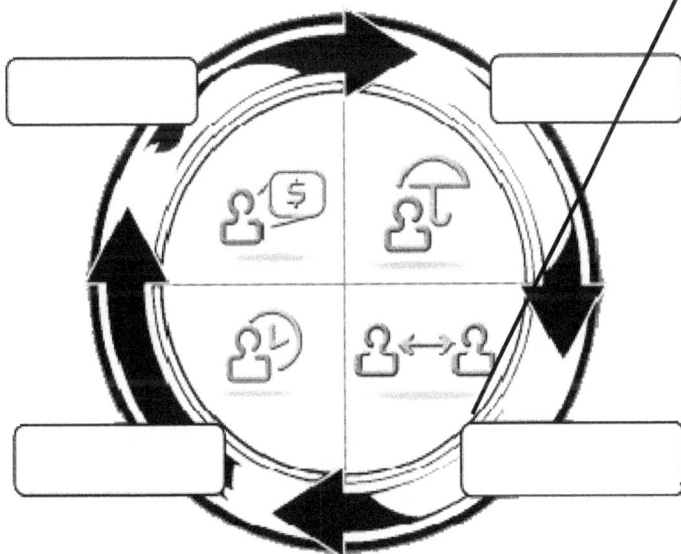

Pathway #2: Communication

This page intentionally blank

Pathway #2: Communication

Effective Communication is...

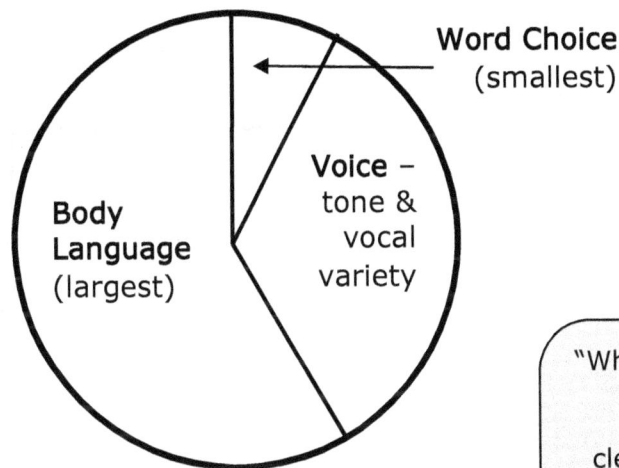

Word Choice (smallest)

Body Language (largest)

Voice – tone & vocal variety

Verbal—Great Orators

_____
_____
_____
_____
_____
_____
_____

> "When two people do not communicate clearly with each other, then what is in their brains and in their hearts might as well stay inside."
> – *Sylvia Henderson*, Founder & CEO, Springboard Training

An Orator . . .

❑ Has a strong command of language; speaks eloquently.
❑ Exudes a self-confident, charismatic physical presence.
❑ Voice is strong and projects out to the audience.
❑ Communicates a focused message repeatedly.
❑ Uses no unnecessary words (um's, ah's, so's, and other filler words).
❑ Makes definitive eye contact with people.
❑ Uses gestures and movement to punctuate, emphasize, and support the presented message.
❑ Tells stories and creates visual images to engage the audience's emotions.
❑ Leads the audience to a unified conclusion and calls for specific action.
❑ Listens to other people and answers questions from their points of view.
❑
❑

CAUTION **ONE WAY**

lan·guage *n.*

- Communication of thoughts and feelings through a system of arbitrary signals, such as voice sounds, gestures, or written symbols.
- Words, their pronunciation, and the methods of combining them used and understood by a community.
- A communications system, including its rules for combining its components, such as words.
- Audible, articulate, meaningful sound as produced by the action of the vocal organs.
- Such a system as used by a nation, people, or other distinct community; often contrasted with dialect.
- A systematic means of communicating ideas or feelings by the use of conventionalized signs, sounds, gestures, or marks having understood meanings.
- The suggestion by objects, actions, or conditions of associated ideas or feelings.
- Body language; kinesics.
- Verbal communication as a subject of study.

References: Dictionary.com and M-W.com (Merriam Webster)

Words

Key points:
- Make appropriate choices. Use words correctly (definitions).
- Speak clearly.
- Enunciate and pronounce properly (regional and nationality influences).

Care to Translate?

Instructions: Read this conversation between two people out loud. What are they saying?

Lo, Zenny buddy rown? Kinyuh kum ovatuh my yows?
Mebbe.
Jeet jet?
Nope. Joo?
Huh-uh. Yawanna goadthanex show?
Kay. Howcumya gotta geddome serly?
Goana grammahz.
Byovah nminit.
Kay. See ya.

How Do You Say…? (Pronunciation)

genuine	preferable	wash	route
theater	government	pen	library
comparable	athlete	February	mischievous

Flexibility Drills (Enunciation)

Syblets

1. Which wristwatches are Swiss wristwatches?

2. Dick twirled the stick athwart the path.

3. Rubber baby-buggy bumpers.

4. Red leather, yellow leather, red leather, yellow leather.

5. The sixth sheik's sixth sheep's sick.

7. If Peter Piper Picked a peck of pickled peppers, Where's the peck of pickled peppers Peter Piper picked?

A Flee, A Fly In A Flue

A flee, a fly in a flue
Were imprisoned, so what could they do?
Said the flee, "Let us fly."
Said the fly, "Let us flee."
So they flew through a flaw in the flue.

Tooting a Flute

A Tudor who tooted a flute
Tried to teach two tooters to toot.
Said the two to the Tudor,
"Is it harder to toot
Or to tutor two tooters to toot?"

"I've learned that people will forget what you said, people will forget what you did, but people will never forget how you made them feel."
– *Maya Angelou*, American Poet

Jargon / Language

Key points:

- Avoid unique jargon and terminology. (If you cannot avoid, define.)
- Language (avoid speaking "over their heads).

> "If it is to be, it is up to me."
> *- William Johnson*

Your Choice of Words—Negative Messages

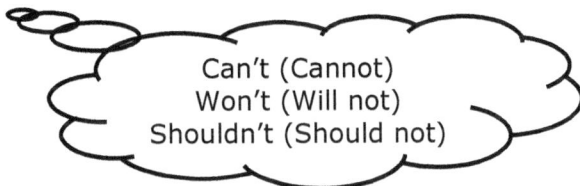

Sunrise

Can't (Cannot)
Won't (Will not)
Shouldn't (Should not)

Can
Will
Try

Sunset

"Because [_____], you can't [_____]."

Negative-to-Positive Messages

1. This won't (will not) be easy.

2. I can't (cannot) do that today.

3. We didn't (did not) see that detail.

4. You shouldn't (should not) approach it like that.

5. They weren't (were not) meant for high achievement.

Additional Reading: Appendix

- "Positive Words," p.70.
- "Confident Comportment," p.71.

> "If you think you are beaten, you are. If you think you dare not, you don't.
> If you like to win and you think you cannot, it is almost certain you won't.
> If you think of losing, you've lost. For, out in the world you find
> Success begins with a [fellows] will . . . It's all in the state of mind.
>
> If you think you're out-classed, you are. Think high so that you rise.
> You've got to be sure of yourself before you can ever win a prize.
> Life's battles do not always go to the stronger or faster [man],
> But sooner or later the one who wins is the one who thinks s/he can."
> *– Author Unknown*

Your Voice = Your Vocal Tool—Vocal Variety

How Can You Hear?

Impatience	Enthusiasm	Empathy
Rudeness	Helpfulness	Sincerity
Friendliness	Misery	Distracted

↝ What comes through when you cannot be seen?

Key points for vocal variety:

Voice (Paralanguage)

- Full volume (from the diaphragm, not the stomach; as low as possible while still "normal").
- Minimize accents, mumbling, "ahs", "ums", "OKs", and "likes."
- Change inflection (vocal variety; emphasis; not monotonous).
- Delivery speed (slow, succinct, and even).
- Pause for effect and to regroup thoughts (silence can be golden).

Why Can't You Do What I Asked?

Why can't you do what I asked? _____

Why **can't** you do what I asked? _____

Why can't **you** do what I asked? _____

Why can't you **do** what I asked? _____

Why can't you do **what** I asked? _____

Why can't you do what **I** asked? _____

Why can't you do what I **asked**? _____

Additional Resources: Appendix

Bibliography of Success Language Resources, p.80.

> "Speech is power: speech is to persuade, to convert, to compel. It is to bring another out of his bad sense into your good sense."
> - *Ralph Waldo Emerson*

> "What lies behind us and what lies before us are small matters compared to what lies within us."
> - *Ralph Waldo Emerson*

Non-Verbal Communication

Key points:

Body Language = Presence
- Use your body to emphasize your message (movement, placement, energy).
- Loosen up (look relaxed).
- Stand or sit with good posture (erect and attentive).
- Look confident even if you don't feel it.
- Smile!

Movement
- Move purposefully (emphasis and effect).
- Eliminate pacing back and forth (distracting).
- Use welcoming gestures (draws people in to you).

Eyes
- Avoid looking out the window, staring at one spot, or looking over the heads of the audience.
- Look at individuals → 5-second rule.
- Remember the back of the room.
- Look up from your notes regularly.

Spatial Relationship *(Proxemics)*

Other parameters: Cultural, gender, ethnic, & life experiences	
	• (Intimate) Zero-to-18 inches (elevator)
	• (Personal) 1.5 feet-to-4 feet (private conversation)
	• (Social) 4 feet-to-12 feet (business calls)
	• (Public) 20 feet or more (public presentations)

Positioning
- Higher than the audience = power; "in charge"; expert.
- Moving/leaning forward = gives attention to; passes control to.
- Moving/leaning backward = moves attention to someone or something else; take back control.

Tips: Body Language

- Make yourself approachable. Smile. Make eye contact. Act "naturally" rather than stiffly or exaggeratedly.
- Honor others' personal space. 1.5feet-to-4feet is considered American culture's personal space.
- The higher plane implies power. Standing when others are sitting implies that the person standing has the power. Sitting higher than others implies the person sitting higher has the power.

Source: "Stuff for Busy People – Proven Techniques You Can Use to be an Effective Communicator." A Pocket Reference Book from Sylvia Henderson. Available from www.SpringboardTraining.com/Invest-Success.

The changes tell you more than "still" snapshots.

Body Language: What Messages?

Casual ____   Patient ___
Alert ____   Defensive ___
Formal ____   Good idea ___
Interested ____   Respectful ___
Secrets ____   Interview ___
Angry ____   Open ___
Disinterested ____   Frustrated ___
Impatient ____   Wary ___
Flirtatious ____   Assertive ___

A   **B**   **C**

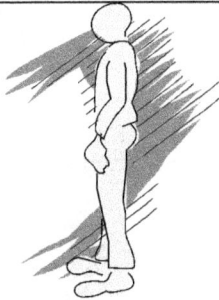   

D   **E**   **F**   **G**   **H**

    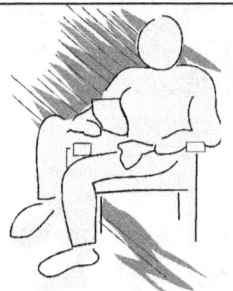

I   **J**   **K**   **L**   **M**

Key points:
- Words, voice, body language, movement, environment, AND physical relationship to others tell the whole story.
- Typically-interpreted negative messages (American society) include patronizing touches, signs of impatience and nervousness, pen and finger tapping, crossed arms, and rolled eyes.
- Typically-interpreted positive messages include good posture, eye contact, genuine smiles, and sincere nods.
- Learn the customs and "hidden messages" of cultures to which you travel and with whom you interact to avoid sending the wrong message with international travel and relationships.

"You can read somebody's attitude–either pleasant or negative–and you can spot that in their body language, their eye contact, and the way they march in."
- *Camille Lavington, Executive Coach*

Active Listening

1	2
	— — — — — —
3	

LISTEN

1-10

Listening Signs

How can you tell?	Barriers

Ten Ways to Listen Well

Stop talking.
You cannot listen if you are talking.

Put the talker at ease.
Help the talker feel he/she is free to talk.

Show that you want to listen.
Look and act interested. Do no read your mail or do other things while the talker is talking. Listen to understand rather than to reply.

Remove distractions.
Do not doodle, tap or shuffle papers. It might be quieter if you shut the door.

Empathize.
Try to put yourself in the speaker's place so that you can see his/her point of view.

Be patient.
Allow plenty of time. Do not interrupt. Do not start for the door or walk away.

Hold your temper.
An angry person gets the wrong meaning from words.

Go easy on argument and criticism.
This puts the talker on the defensive. She/he may stop speaking, close up, or get angry. Do not argue; even if you win, you lose.

Ask questions.
This encourages the talker and shows you are listening. It helps to develop points further.

Stop talking!
This is first and last because all other "rules" depend on it. You cannot do a good listening job while you are talking.

– From Olde Manners Booklette (Author Unknown)

"Nature has given us one tongue, but two ears that we may hear from others twice as much as we speak."
– Epictetus (Ancient Greek Philosopher)

Written Communications

	Formal	Informal
⟿ What constitutes?		
⟿ Characteristics?		
⟿ When appropriate to use?		

Comments About & Guidelines for Electronic Communications

Here to stay! Deal with it.

Z THS TH WY 2 RIT 4 BZNZ CMUNCTZ? ROTFL!

Reference: NetLingo.com

☞ Texting
☞ Re-tweet
☞ Posts
☞ Links
☞ Feeds
☞ FAQs

Changes / additions daily!

Communications Styles

Assessment and category options:

- Listener; Creative; Doer; Thinker
- Expresser; Driver; Relater; Analytical
- Passive; Assertive; Aggressive
- Action; Process; Idea; People (*Scranton.edu*)
- Open; Reserved; Direct; Indirect
- Myers-Briggs Type Indicator™ (*Katharine Cook Briggs and Isabel Briggs Myers*—Extraversion/Introversion; Sensing/iNtuition; Thinking/Feeling; Judging/Perceiving)
- Communications Jungle™ (*Business Training Works*—Lions; Peacocks; Turtles; Doves)
- Keirsey Temperament Sorter™ (*David Keirsey*—Artisans; Guardians; Idealists; Rationals)
- DiSC Profile™ (*William Moulton Marston Ph.D*—Dominance; Influence; Steadiness; Conscientiousness)

Many more!
Search: "communication* + styles"

Additional Resources: Appendix

- "Communications Styles: A Self-Assessment," p.81.
- "Written Communications: Perhaps You Might Reconsider," p.87.

Key points:

- Each of us has at least one dominant communications style.
- Different people have different styles of communication.
- To communicate effectively, we must understand how to "reach" the other person through their style(s).
- Assessments create boxes for us, yet we seldom truly operate within "our box." Be flexible.
- Effective leaders have a "communications saddlebag" with several alternative tools that produce their desired outcome.

Well-Intentioned Messages

When they say…	I hear / feel…	Perhaps they mean…	So I will…

Additional Resource:

Article: "Well-Intentioned Messages: It's For Your Own Good!".

Source: www.springboardtraining.com/topics-by-category/interpersonal-communications/well-intentioned-messages.

The article offers suggestions on how to deal with such messages.

> "Unsolicited advice is what you get when you give someone who isn't listening, counseling they didn't ask for, offering recommendations you probably aren't even following yourself."
> – Brad Bollenbach

Key points (on the receiving end):
- Try to discern from where the advice comes. ("I just want to help you." Friendliness. Excitement of learning something new and wanting to share. Needing to be needed. Ego. Dominance. Judgment. Tired of hearing you complain.)
- Decide if you want the advice. (Political ramifications at work. A great idea. Safety or security.)
- If welcome—"Thank you."
- If accepted yet not taken—"Thank you. I'll take that into consideration."
- To establish a boundary—"I'm glad that works for you. There are so many different ways of doing things."

Key points (on the giving end): See "Giving and Receiving Feedback," p.40.

> "We should make sure that our own house is in order before we give advice to others."
> – Aesop's Fables

© www.SpringboardTraining.com

Giving and Receiving Feedback

Guide for Giving Feedback

Request for conversation	*"I'd like to talk to you about ..."*
Describe observable behavior	*"____, when you ..."* *"I notice you ..."* *"When I hear you saying ..."*
Tell how behavior affects you	*"I feel confused, angry, pleased* *> because the group is ..."* *> others are ..."* *> at that moment, I am ..."* *> because we ..."*
Tell why you are affected	*"I feel this way because I* *> am concluding that ..."* *> believe that ..."* *> am assuming you ..."*
Allow response	*"How do you see the situation?"* *"Can you help me understand your point of view?"*

- **Focus on the behavior, not the person.** Use full "I" statements. Rather than say "You just don't seem to care!", try "I am disappointed when your monthly reports are late. When your report is missing, I cannot complete my summary."

- **Be wary of using "always" and "never."** Be specific about how often the behavior occurs.

- **Give feedback immediately.** Timely feedback is most effective and valuable to the receiver. If immediately is not an option, make the feedback session as soon after the situation as possible.

- **Focus on what is said or done rather than why.** Address behaviors and how to improve (or change) them, as well as how they affect you.

- **Be sensitive.** The time, place, and listener's state-of-mind impact the outcome. Use a private place if necessary.

- **Identify one issue at a time.** Try to focus on the issue that gives results quickly.

- **Ask the person receiving your feedback to paraphrase** what he/she heard you say.

- **Practice active listening skills.**

- **Check your intentions.** Make sure you genuinely intend to help—either the person or the environment / situation.

Notes

Receiving Feedback

Say to the speaker:
- "Did I hear you say ...?"
- "Do you mean ...?"

Paraphrase comments you think you heard.

Actions—raised eyebrow, quizzical look, smile, fidget, silence—send signals to the speaker.

Defensive responses:
- "No!"
- "Yes but..."
- "Oh, it was nothing."
- "The reason that I ..."
- "I was only doing my job."
- "You didn't understand that ..."

"Advice is seldom welcome; and those who want it the most seem to like it the least."
– Earl of Chesterfield

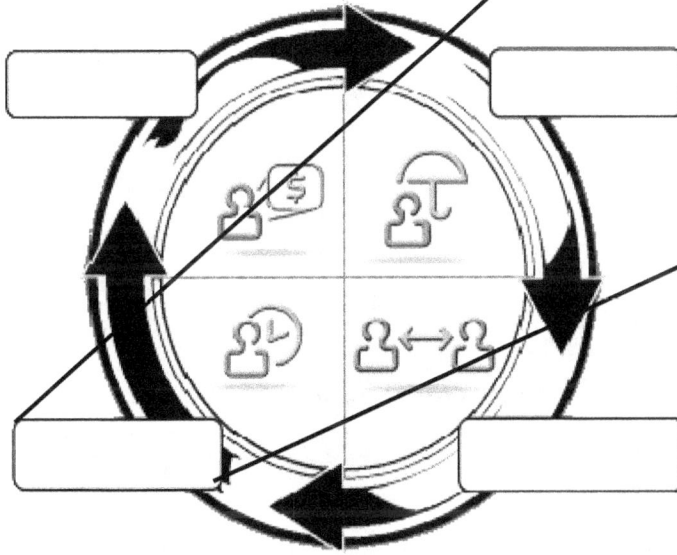

Pathway #3: Behavior

This page intentionally blank

Pathway #3: Behavior

Work Ethic *n.* A set of values based on the moral virtues of hard work and diligence.

Source: The American Heritage® Dictionary of the English Language.

- Characteristics of "positive work ethic"

- Multi-tasking
  - Seems to vary generationally.
  - Mistake-prone.
  - Manage multiple demands.
  - Leadership competency.
- Completed staff work
  - Meets deadlines.
  - Thorough and accurate.
- Quality work product
  - Spelling and grammar are correct.
  - Context is appropriate.
  - Edited, proof-read, and reviewed for content correctness by different sets of eyes.
  - Looks good; presents well (clean; neat; stain-free.)

↝ Example of your environment?

Notes

Resources: Work Ethic

(1)

The Work Ethic Site.
Department of Workforce Education,
Leadership, & Social Foundations.
The University of Georgia.
Athens, GA 30602-4809
http://www.coe.uga.edu/workethic/ .

(2)

Springboard iNFO_NOTE©:
Work Ethics
A four-page paper on work ethics and work.
Request a copy at www.Springboard Training.com/contact.

" The point of life is not to arrive at your grave safe and sound, but to skid in sideways, out of control screaming, 'Whoa...What a ride!'"
- *Author unknown*

Timeliness: "On Time", Every Time

START TIMES				
: __M			Actual appointment time.
: __M			Your appointment time (actual – 10 minutes).
: M	-	min	
: M	-	min	
: M	-	min	
: M	-	min	
: M	-	min	
: M	-	min	
: M	-	min	
: M	-	min	

Key point: "10 minutes early is 'on-time'." – *William A. Henderson*

Additional Resources: Appendix

- Resources for Time, Calendars, and Scheduling, p.83.
- "Time Management Tips," p.84

> "What we love to do we find time to do."
> — *John L. Spalding*

Time / Motion Study

Actions	7A	8A	9A	10A	11A	Noon	1P	2P	3P	4P	5P	6P	7P
Get ready for work													
Commute / travel													
Coffee; catch up													
E-mail													
Telephone													
Paperwork; reports													
Meetings													

"Where does the time disappear?" If you find yourself asking this question after your best intent to do a better job managing your time, identify where your "time disappears." A time/motion study causes you to document how you spend your day in small time increments. When you add up the time spent on various activities within a day, week, and month you find where and how you spend your time. You will identify what actions need re-evaluating and control. The above chart is an example of such a time/motion study for one day in the life of an office supervisor.

Overcome Procrastination, Distractions, and Other Barriers to Manage Time Effectively

Consider these recommendations to gain better control of your time.

- Review your long-term and intermediate goals often. Keep them listed where you can see them.
- Continually eliminate unnecessary tasks not related to your goals or to maintaining a balanced lifestyle.
- Take advantage of your natural cycles (highest and lowest energy and creativity levels for you in the mornings, afternoons, evenings, late nights). Schedule difficult activities for when you are sharpest.
- Learn to say "no" to people, including spouses, friends, children, parents, colleagues, and bosses.
- Reward yourself for effective time management.
- Solicit cooperation from those around you. Let people know about your efforts to manage time.
- Avoid setting yourself up to fail. Be realistic about what you can accomplish within a certain amount of time, as well as your total demands and commitments. Work towards an individualized approach to managing time that makes sense for you.
- Put schedules, priorities, and plans on paper. Recording things is helpful in and of itself (the process of recording). When you see them written down, you see how realistic (or unrealistic) they are.
- Be spontaneous, occasionally.

Time Sayings
Time flies when you're having fun.
A stitch in time saves nine.
Time is on your side.

Interruptions: Emergency, But Is It Yours?

"Before you leave, would you please handle *[fill in the blank]*? It's an emergency!"

Usually you hear these words just before you leave the office for the day or go on your week's vacation. Next time you hear these words, ask yourself, "Whose emergency?" Someone else's poor planning does not your emergency make.

Your day is full of "situations." Plan and communicate well to effectively manage most of the challenges you encounter. When someone brings you what, to them, is an emergency when it is not necessarily your own, avoid making the emergency your own.

- Make it a habit to ask questions when situations are brought to you. Define exact due dates and dependencies.
- What effect will your action – and inaction – have on other areas of the business or other people?
- Does someone you report to – a manager or client – deem the situation an emergency? Do you care?
- What other commitments do you balance for which this additional one is just too much to effectively handle?

When "It's an emergency", ask questions to determine whether the situation really is YOUR emergency.

Work-Life Balance

A typical time management mistake is to ignore or overlook a balanced lifestyle. Your overall health and wellness requires attention to six important life areas:

- **Physical** (exercise; nutrition; sleep).
- **Intellectual** (culture; aesthetics).
- **Social** (intimacy; social relationships).
- **Career** (school; career; goal-directed work).
- **Emotional** (expressed feelings; desires).
- **Spiritual** (quest for meaning in – and of – life).

It is unrealistic to expect to have a designated set of activities in each of these areas every day. If, however, you fail to attend to one or more areas at all, you risk ignoring important parts of yourself. Attending to one area may also help you in other areas. For example, if you set aside time for exercise, you improve how you function overall and better manage your stress. If you take time to foster your intellectual growth, you gain new perspectives on life, experience different kinds of pleasure, and are better able to focus on your goals.

Syndicated column. © Sylvia Henderson. All rights reserved.

Schedule Sheet: A Tool for Balance

"We all have the same amount of time: 24 hours in a day, 7 days in a week, 12 months in a year. It is what we do with the time that matters."
— *Sylvia Henderson*

Workplace Etiquette: Getting Along With Others

Pet Peeves: Minor annoyances that you identify as particularly annoying to you, to a greater degree than others may find them. Examples may include poor table manners, sloppy kitchen hygiene, smoking, grammatical errors in written passages, inconsiderate co-workers, obnoxious behavior on public transportation, or loud gum smacking. Unfortunately, there are so many more.

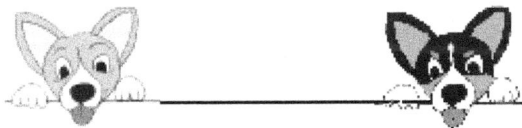

Etiquette guidelines: private behaviors

❑
❑
❑
❑
❑

Etiquette guidelines: public behaviors

❑
❑
❑
❑

Etiquette guidelines: environment

❑
❑
❑
❑

Common Courtesy…Uncommon

"In the old days people would—" How many of us have heard this statement from our parents' generation? It seems that acts of common courtesy are mired in "correctness" movements and forgotten in the hectic pace of life.

These small acts of courtesy remain appropriate and are deemed as considerate actions regardless of generation or gender.

- Hold the door open for the person following directly behind you.
- Open the door for someone whose hands are full.
- Give up your seat when someone clearly needs to sit more than you do.
- Greet people—especially those you see regularly—with a friendly "Hello"—and look at them while doing so.

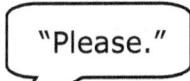

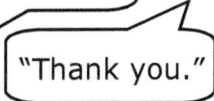

Syndicated column. © Sylvia Henderson. All rights reserved.

"Please."

"Thank you."

"Courtesy is as much a mark of a gentle[man] as courage."
- *Theodore Roosevelt*

Multiple Generations in the Workplace

Paradigms:

- Virtual workplace
- 24/7 availability
- Regular and exponential technological advances
- Instant and viral messages
- Social media ("social" w/o face-to-face contact)
- International presence and "reach"
- Major generational shifts (outbound; inbound)
- Knowledge base transfer (or loss)
- Challenges to "status quo"
- Skepticism of business ethics
- "More to life than work" attitude
- Civic consciousness
- Immediate and direct value and worth
- Diminished "thinking" educational experiences (prep to pass the tests)

Veterans (Traditionals)	1922-1945
Baby Boomers	1946-1964
Generation X	1965-1980
Millennials (Generation Y/Why?)	1981-2000

	Direct Influences	Consequences	Solutions
Veterans / Traditionals			
Baby Boomers			
Generation X			
Millennials			
Next?			

"Parents often talk about the younger generation as if they didn't have anything to do with it."
– Haim Ginott

Manners Matter

Social and Professional Protocol: The Handshake

The correct way to shake hands (in America) applies to both men and women. Connect the "v" between the thumb and index finger of your right hand with the "v" between the thumb and index finger of the other person's right hand. Give one to two "pumps" and make eye contact. Use a firm grasp without competing for whose handshake is the strongest. Avoid sweaty palms by washing your hands using soap, and drying thoroughly before the anticipated handshake.

The person initiating the handshake is typically the person in control–which is what you want. A good handshake lasts for about 3-to-4 seconds. If you offer a handshake and it is refused, withdraw your hand. You know you followed protocol while the other person is ungracious.

Source: tips4me.com/tips/etiquette and protocolconsultants.com

> "Respect for ourselves guides our morals; respect for others guides our manners."
> - *Laurence Sterne*

Key points:
- Social graces reflect your professional values.
- Business decisions are made in social situations (networking events; golf course; meals.)
- You never know whom you will meet in a public space at any time, or at another job.
- Introduce people by rank or position in your organization; most familiar (to you) to least; client first.
- Know the name norms. Can you use first names, or do you use "Mr. / Ms. / Mrs.?"
- Use business cards. Exchange them. Avoid discarding someone's card within their presence.
- Dress appropriately. Doing so communicates that you pay attention to detail, are concerned about your customers' reactions, have good organizational skills, and provide a better product.
- Spend money on one well-made, quality suit that fits well rather than many "cheap" suits.
- There is no place or time for derogatory language.
- It's an international business environment. Take the time to learn your client's language, time zones, working schedules, holidays, and food customs (table manners, use of implements, etc.)
- Take a business etiquette class.

Additional Reading: Appendix

- "Social and Professional Protocol: Telephone Etiquette," p.86.
- "Social and Professional Protocol: E-Mail," p.87.
- "Social and Professional Protocol: Communicating in Writing," p.88.
- "Meetings," p.89.
- "Social and Professional Protocol: Let's Eat Out (Dining Etiquette)," p.91.

Take Initiative

Why ask to be empowered? You already are. Taking initiative is how you demonstrate your empowerment.

Tips for Taking Initiative

Key points:

- Be proactive. Anticipate problems at your level and solve them before they grow.
- Help your boss look good.
- Be your own advocate. Present clear messages; make the "ask"; support with the appropriate communications style.

Additional Reading: Appendix
"Initiative—Be a 'Leader of One'," p.85.

> "If you want to stand out, don't be different; be outstanding."
> - *Mae West, Actress*

---

initiative *n.*

1. an introductory act or step; leading action: "to take the initiative."
2. readiness and ability in initiating action; enterprise.
3. one's personal, responsible decision: to act on one's own initiative.

How does "initiative" relate to...

↝ Excellence?

↝ Service?

↝ Empowerment?

↝ Advancement?

Important Qualities for Job Candidates

Summary of a "Job Outlook Survey" conducted by the National Association of Colleges and Employers (NACE)

NACE annually asks employers to rate the importance of a variety of skills and abilities. The results consistently reveal the same qualities as important to employers.

Qualities (Skills and Abilities)	*Importance Rating (On A Scale of 1-to-5)*
• Communications skills	4.6
• Strong work ethic	4.6
• Teamwork skills	4.5
• Initiative	4.4
• Interpersonal skills	4.4
• Problem-solving skills	4.4
• Analytical skills	4.3
• Flexibility / adaptability	4.2
• Computer skills	4.1
• Technical skills	4.1
• Detail-oriented	4.0
• Organizational skills	4.0

> "You don't have to be great to start, but you have to start to be great."
> – *Zig Ziglar*

Making Decisions

The basic structure of a decision-making process involves:

1. Define the problem.
2. Collect necessary information.
3. Develop options.
4. Devise a plan.
5. Execute the plan.
6. Follow-up (analyze; evaluate; adjust).

Commonly-Used Decision Models

- Simple pros and cons (+ / - columns; PMI Analysis)
- Many factors; multiple choices; identify and weigh the best options (Pareto Analysis; Grid Analysis; SWOT Analysis; Force Field Analysis; Cost/Benefit Analysis)
- Identify causes and effects; gather information (Starbursting; Mind Mapping; 5Whys; "So What")
- Consider everyone's points of view (Six Thinking Hats; Stepladder Technique)

Decision-Making Tips

Key points:

- Decide quickly; change slowly.
- Make your own decisions; be your own person.
- Seek expert counsel, then commit.
- Take responsibility.
- Avoid bogging down in "what ifs."
- Assess and update. Learn from errors.
- Keep in mind your decision is within the frame you choose.
- Personal values and ethics rule.
- Do your best and be okay with it.

Additional Resources: Critical Thinking

- **Aha!!! Learning To Think Critically And Creatively: Techniques For Sparking Ideas, Solving Problems, And Rethinking The Status Quo**
  Author: Kate Zabrinski. ISBN #978-1935425014.
  www.BusinessTrainingWorks.com
- **Mind Tools: Essential Skills for an Excellent Career**
  www.MindTools.com

> "It requires a very unusual mind to undertake the analysis of the obvious."
> *– Alfred N Whitehead (1861-1947)*

Captions?

Teamwork: Challenge

_____

_____

_____

_____

_____

_____

_____

_____

_____

_____

_____

_____

_____

_____

Aesop's Fable: The Belly and the Members

One fine day it occurred to the Members of the Body that they were doing all the work and the Belly was having all the food. So they held a meeting, and after a long discussion, decided to strike work until the Belly consented to take on its proper share of the work. For a day or two, the Hands refused to take the food, the Mouth refused to receive it, and the Teeth had no work to do. But after a day or two the Members began to find that they themselves were not in a very active condition: the Hands could hardly move, and the Mouth was all parched and dry, while the Legs were unable to support the rest. So thus they found that even the Belly in its dull quiet way was doing necessary work for the Body, and that all must work together or the Body will go to pieces.

… And the moral of the story is: All must work together.

The text of Aesop's Fables is public domain.

> "The ultimate victory in competition is derived from the inner satisfaction of knowing you have done your best and you have gotten the most out of what you had to give."
> - *Howard Cosell*

Teamwork—Competition and Cooperation

When I think of or experience teams—be they sports, hobby, volunteer, or otherwise—they work…

Positively – towards a common goal – by:	*Negatively* – against themselves – to the detriment of achieving a common goal by:

Leaders of teams do these things to positively support and carry-out their leadership roles and positions:

> "The healthiest competition occurs when average people win by investing above average effort."
> - Colin Powell

Additional Readings and Resources: Appendix

- "Who is Aesop and What are 'Aesop's Fables?'" p.79.
- Resources for Teamwork and Working Well With Others, p.83.
- "Teamwork: Mentoring Others," p.85.

Self-Growth and Life-Long Learning

Suggested Resources:

- Management / Leadership: www.12manage.com –and– www.MindTools.com
- Success / Personal Development / Motivation: www.SelfGrowth.com (*articles; videos; audio; experts; products*) –and– www.tstn.com (*The Success Training Network*)
- Work-Life / Career: www.SpringboardTraining.com –and– www.BusinessTrainingWorks.com

> "A person who graduated yesterday and stops studying today is uneducated tomorrow."
> – *Unknown*

Get Along With "Difficult People" In Difficult Situations – Manage and Mitigate Conflict

Multiple Generations	General Tips

Multiple Generations

- ***Learn to "pass the torch."*** Identify what you can pass on to a less-experienced workforce. Then provide guidance to help people learn.

- ***Adjust to an information-rich environment.*** Create and contribute to a culture where people share valuable information and explain reasoning behind decisions to sense of community.

- ***Accumulate wisdom.*** Open your mind to experience and guidance. Use each other's strengths. Younger workers are typically technologically-savvy. Older workers are typically corporate savvy.

- ***Build credibility and trustworthiness.*** Keep promises. Demonstrate patience and willingness to learn.

- ***Forge developmental alliances.*** Seek mentors. Encourage and teach protégés.

- ***Remember that work is evolutionary.*** Older workers had opportunities to transform the workplace. Younger workers have similar expectations.

- ***Appreciate and foster the need for independence.*** Avoid micromanaging. Earn the "right" to be independent. Take responsibility and prove you can handle it.

- ***Focus on community to earn loyalty.*** Foster work/life balance to give meaning to life. When people feel valued they give more of themselves.

- ***Keep in mind that there will always be a "younger generation."*** Others will follow and experience the environment that you create.

📑 **Reference Scenarios: Appendix**
"Pathways Scenarios: Set 3," p.96.

> "Eventually we will find (mostly in retrospect, of course) that we can be very grateful to those people who have made life most difficult for us."
> – Ayya Khema

General Tips

- ***Forgive.*** At our very core most of us are "good people." Our judgment gets clouded and we say hurtful things. Ask yourself, "What is it about this situation or person that I can seek to understand and forgive?"

- ***Wait it out.*** Emotionally charged responses seldom get us the results we want; they only add fuel to fires. Allow time to cool off. You can write an emotionally charged missive to someone and not send it. Give yourself time to calm down before responding, if you choose to respond at all.

- ***Ask yourself, "Does it really matter if I am right?"*** If you find yourself arguing for the sake of being right, ask, "Does it matter if I am right?" If yes, then ask, "Why do I need to be right? What will I gain?"

- ***Stop talking about it.*** Stop giving difficulties energy. Stop thinking and talking about them. Avoid repeating other people's stories.

- ***Be in their shoes.*** Put yourself in another person's position to consider how you may have hurt their feelings. Doing so gives you a new perspective and may help you develop compassion for the other person.

- ***Look for the lessons.*** Difficult situations are not lost if we can take away from them lessons that help us grow and become better people. Negative scenarios provide hidden gifts in the form of lessons. Find the lesson(s).

- ***List the things in your life most important to you.*** Then ask yourself, "How will reacting to this person or situation contribute to the things that matter most to me?" Your answer will help you determine your next move.

- ***Express yourself appropriately.*** Learn how to give and receive feedback effectively. Then, practice.

- ***Be honest with yourself as to whether you are better off making a change.*** Occasionally, situations grow beyond "resolution in place." You may need to make the difficult decision to leave your current environment for one more conducive to your needs and goals.

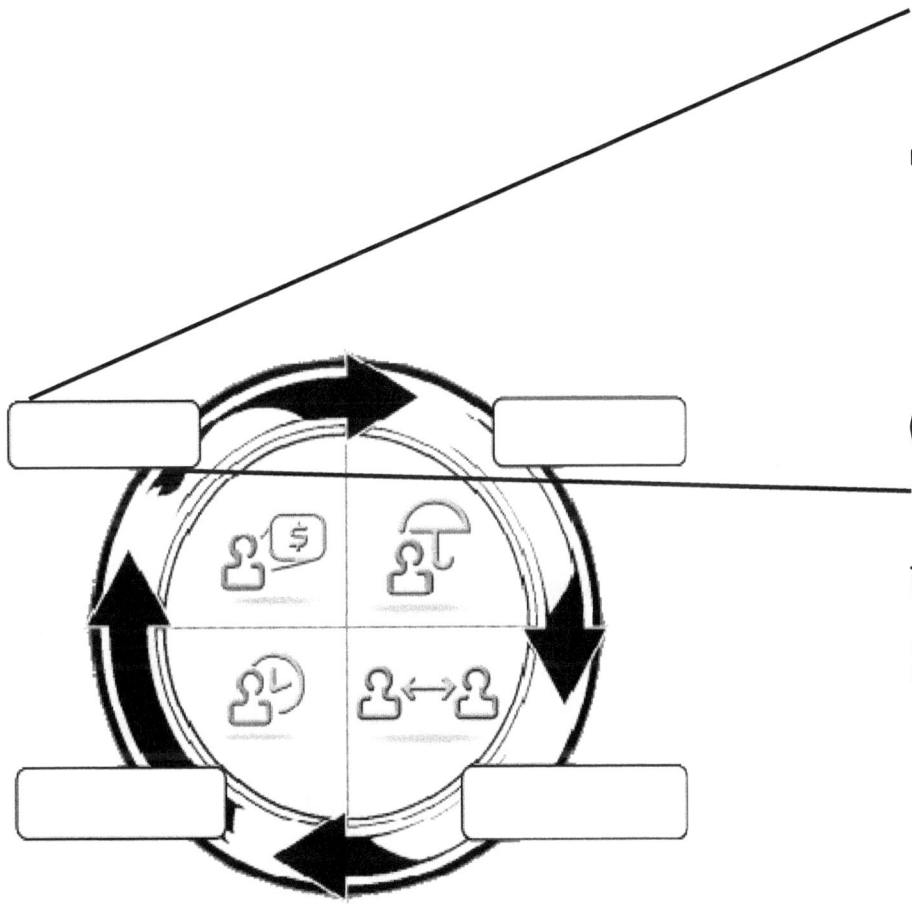

Pathway #4: Results

This page intentionally blank

Pathway #4: Results

Key points:

- "Busyness" = doing. Achievement / accomplishment = completing.
- There is a direct correlation between "results" and "SMART goals."
- Effective and fair performance plans might better be called results guides.
- Being busy, costs. Achieving results, pays.

> "First say to yourself what you would be; and then do what you have to do."
> – *Epictetus*

Philanthropy: Giving Back

Keep your **MoTR** running.	What can you offer to others?

Key points:

- "Success" bears a civic responsibility.
- **Mo**ney ⎫
- **T**ime ⎬ Everyone has – and can offer – at least one!
- **R**esources ⎭
- Long-term makes the difference. Integrate philanthropy into your life plan.

📄 Suggested Resources: Giving Back

- National Database for Volunteerism (Volunteers of America): www.VOA.org
- The President's Volunteer Service Award – Springboard Training is a qualifying organization
  - www.SpringboardTraining.com/About-ST/Giving-Back
  - www.PresidentialServiceAwards.gov
- The Foundation Center: cnl.foundationcenter.org
- Your local Chambers of Commerce

> Yes, this is a correct URL.
> CNL = Catalog of Nonprofit Literature
> (a searchable database).

> "We must not, in trying to think about how we can make a big difference, ignore the small daily differences we can make that, over time, add up to big differences we often cannot foresee."
> - *Marian Wright Edelman*

Being Noticed: Your Achievements?

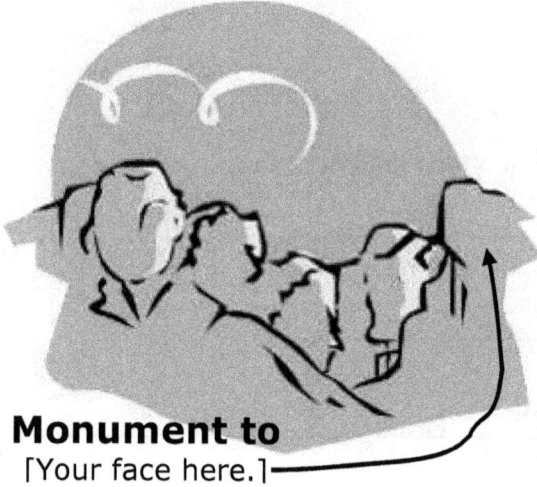

Monument to
⌐Your face here.⌐

(Mount Rushmore National Monument–South Dakota, USA)

What words will be read?

SMART Goals...Know When You "Achieve Success"

S =
M =
A =
R =
T =

Key points:
- Use action verbs.
- Write them down. Say them out loud.
- Keep them visible.
- Have an accountability partner.
- Identify times; milestones.
- Define your vision for and purpose of each goal.
- Determine realistic action items. Take action.
- Reward yourself at milestones.
- Maintain a "life 'to do' list" (bucket list).
- Never finish (not over 'til you're over).
- Ensure your legacy.

What will you do <u>now</u> to make it happen?

How will we know?

Memorial Trivia: *Mount Rushmore National Monument – South Dakota. Sculptor: Gutzon Borglum. The monument is called the Shrine of Democracy. It took 14 years and $1million to create, and features the faces of four American presidents; George Washington, Thomas Jefferson, Theodore Roosevelt, and Abraham Lincoln. Backdrop: Black Hills of South Dakota. Faces are 60-feet high, 500 feet up.*

Recognition and Appreciation—Accentuate the Positive

Observable _____

Talent or skill _____

Impact (on self or organization) _____

Symbol of appreciation _____

- Proud (of oneself, or others) → **proud** adj 1: feeling self-respect or pleasure in something by which you measure your self-worth; or being a reason for pride; "proud parents"; "proud of one's accomplishments"; "a proud moment"; "proud to serve your country"; "a proud name."

- Prideful → **prideful** adj 1: having or showing arrogant superiority to and disdain for those one views as unworthy; "some economists are disdainful of their colleagues in other social disciplines"; "haughty aristocrats"; "his lordly manners were offensive"; "walked with a prideful swagger."

Reference: Dictionary.com

> "If you do things well, do them better. Be daring, be first, be different, be just."
> - *Anita Roddick*

Express Yourself

At the very least…

That wasn't so hard, was it?

Take Action!

- ⚡ How does it all tie together?
- ⚡ How does it apply to me / us?

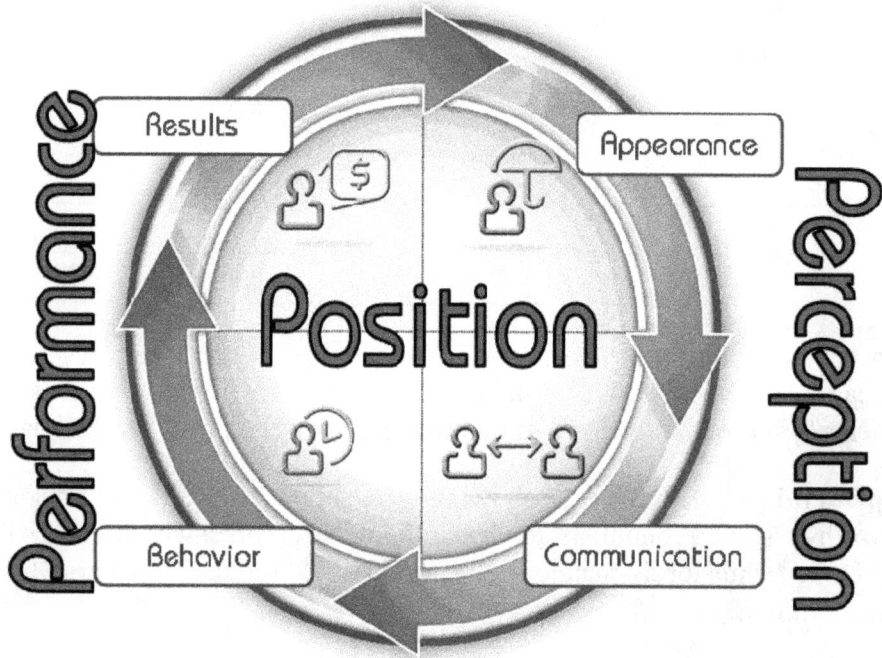

Results

Appearance

Performance

Perception

Position

Behavior

Communication

Here at _____

PATHWAYS	⚡ Appearance	
	⚡ Communication	
	⚡ Behavior	
	⚡ Results	
SUCCESS FORMULA	⚡ Perception	
	⚡ Performance	
	⚡ Position	

"If the road to success is under construction, become a construction worker."
- Unknown

Tell The World About It

- Headline – catchy and meaningful.
- 2-to-3 paragraphs.
- <u>Your words</u> about this program.

Benefits:

What's in it for you?

Primary message you take from the program.

Why take the time?

Pathways to Positioning: A Different Kind of Summary

```
M J H N D V S I Y C J D A S M I J F H R
Q Y C S R O I V A H E B P S I H Y E P N
R K K R O W M A E T F H I E N B G E R Q
V E S U P P O R T G Y L T R D R R D A Y
Y V S Q D L S E S S A B I T S C O B T U
H J N U E F U N I N N M R S E L O A I B
V I I A L Q G C O E O J I P T J M C M Q
N L E V I T A I T I N I T Y S E I K E D
L S P T L L S T A T T I T U D I N A L G
T N E M H S I L P M O C C A M O G I I S
B A R V E R B A L N H O A E M W N D N E
U P S F W K W N A A M R C R A R O O E G
B P O I Q U C R N M H N H B T Q I I S K
L R N L H S T G U E A T I I T S T F S Z
P E A R W I E N P M W B E I I H I J F Y
X C L N F A I O R O P O V C R F N D L A
N I A A D C S O R T L V E K E R G D S W
D A C M A I F G B I D D M I V R O M U H
H T T T R F P W O R K E T H I C P B T
S I I I E L W P B N E C N A R A E P P A
P O O P E C N A L A B Y T I I I R B M P
N N N S J U B Q S L L C N J E H G U F J
```

Find the following words in the above puzzle. Within the puzzle the words may be oriented up, down, or criss-cross; backwards or forwards. Some words share the letters of other words as they criss-cross each other. All of the words in the list below are in this puzzle.

ACCOMPLISHMENT
ACHIEVEMENT
AFFIRMATIONS
APPEARANCE
APPRECIATION
ARTIFACTS
ATTIRE
ATTITUDINAL
BALANCE
BEHAVIOR
BRAND

CHANGE
COMMUNICATION
DECISIONS
DISTRACTIONS
EMOTIONAL
ETIQUETTE
FEEDBACK
GROOMING
HUMOR
IMAGE
INITIATIVE

LISTENING
MINDSET
PATHWAY
PERCEPTION
PERFORMANCE
PERSONALACTION
PHYSICAL
POSITION
PROFESSIONALISM
RECOGNITION
RESULTS

SELFGROWTH
STRESS
SUPPORT
TEAMWORK
TIMELINESS
VERBAL
WORKETHIC
WRITTEN

Notes

_____

_____

_____

_____

_____

_____

_____

_____

_____

_____

_____

_____

_____

_____

_____

_____

_____

_____

_____

_____

To-Do List

☐ Recommend to management / decision-makers to contract this vendor to conduct programs and secure professional development resources for your organization.

☐

☐

☐

☐

Personal Action Contract© ➲ P•A•C

I, _____ will:

> Luke: All right, I'll give it a try.
> Yoda: No! Try not! Do or do not. There is no try.
> – *Yoda, to Luke Skywalker, Star Wars Episode V: The Empire Strikes Back*

What:	By (When):	☐
	Why:	
Want / Need:	Who:	
Whoa!		

What:	By (When):	☐
	Why:	
Want / Need:	Who:	
Whoa!		

This page intentionally blank

Appendix

Appendix: Resources for Further Study

- Assessments
- Scenarios
- Readings
- Job Aids
- Resource References

This page intentionally blank

Professionalism—Self-Assessment

Instructions: Mark the circle in the column that best represents how you view yourself for each statement. *(One circle per statement.)*

	Never	Sometimes	Consistently (Most Times)
1) I understand my organization's goals.	(0)	(1)	(2)
2) I have opinions about where the organization should be, and what management needs to do to get there.	(0)	(1)	(2)
3) I take initiative by starting things on my own.	(0)	(1)	(2)
4) I find fulfillment in what I do.	(0)	(1)	(2)
5) I do not mind making mistakes as long as I am not chastised for doing so.	(0)	(1)	(2)
6) I give feedback to others, when appropriate.	(0)	(1)	(2)
7) I maintain a positive attitude.	(0)	(1)	(2)
8) I am recognized for doing my job well.	(0)	(1)	(2)
9) I find someone to cover for me, and make sure my responsibilities are handled when I have to be away.	(0)	(1)	(2)
10) I speak with my boss—and/or others in positions I want to attain—to learn what I need to do in order to advance in my organization.	(0)	(1)	(2)
11) I do a good job and work hard to be a solid performer.	(0)	(1)	(2)
12) I am well groomed and dress professionally (within my organization's guidelines).	(0)	(1)	(2)
13) I believe I have been in my position long enough, and work hard enough, to merit a raise or promotion.	(0)	(1)	(2)
14) When I take on a task, I ask questions to clarify expectations, then do what I need to do complete the task.	(0)	(1)	(2)
15) I cope with and work through change.	(0)	(1)	(2)
16) I do everything that is expected of me.	(0)	(1)	(2)
17) I can be trusted to handle money.	(0)	(1)	(2)
18) I am honest when people ask me about something.	(0)	(1)	(2)
19) I follow through with my commitments and promises.	(0)	(1)	(2)
20) I am loyal to and show respect for my boss (manager, supervisor, other).	(0)	(1)	(2)
21) I have the ability to motivate and direct others.	(0)	(1)	(2)
22) I am a team player and work well with others.	(0)	(1)	(2)

© www.SpringboardTraining.com

Never	Sometimes	Consistently
		(Most Times)

Scoring Instructions: A. Total each column by adding the (numbers) checked for each column.

Example: ⊗ (2) + ⊗ (2) + ⊗ (1) = 5

↘ ↘ ↘

B. Then, Add the numbers in these three boxes together, and put the total number in the large box below. ↘

SPRINGBOARD
TRAINING
"Your springboard to personal and professional development!"

Total Score:

0-to-11	12-to-25	26-to-40	41-to-44
What? And you're still employed?	Consider a serious change in your attitude and work habits to remain in your current position.	You are demonstrating some of the professional behaviors that show that you have a positive work ethic.	Great! You are doing what is most-likely expected of you in your job.

This self-assessment is a program tool rather than a validated employment profile instrument. Yet, the statements you rate represent thoughts, words, and values that supervisors, managers, and career specialists note repeatedly as characteristics of employees who do exactly what is expected of them in their current jobs. Much more is typically expected of employees to even be considered for advancement, raises, and bonuses (positioning).

Continue your personal and professional development pursuits throughout your life. **Examine your attitude. Consider your level of excellence. Acquire tools** that develop your knowledge, build your skills, and shape your attitude towards professionalism, work ethics, and leadership excellence at www.SpringboardTraining.com. Programs, resources, and educational tools are your *"springboard to personal and professional development!"*

Examine your behaviors and attitudes as you consider your opportunities for additional responsibilities and advancement:

- ☐ Do you help others learn, develop themselves, and succeed?
- ☐ Do you volunteer to lead projects (or groups of people) and follow-through with your commitments?
- ☐ Do you speak, write, and listen well?
- ☐ Do you present yourself at the level to which you seek advancement?
- ☐ Do you offer to speak in front of groups of people, or to make presentations to your management?
- ☐ Do you take initiative and seek opportunities to take risks, stand out from the rest of your peers, or do/say things that go beyond the norm of your environment…in a positive way?
- ☐ Do you learn from your mistakes?
- ☐ Do you contribute to setting the direction of, or procedures for, your department, agency, or organization?

When you demonstrate some—or all—of the above behaviors and attitudes, you **position yourself for being considered** for advancement and recognition.

Source: Springboard Training. www.SpringboardTraining.com

Guidelines for Attire at Receptions, Presentations and Information Sessions

Present yourself in the most conservative and professional manner you can regardless of the "code."

Code: Business / Professional

Both Men and Women: Wear a business suit.

Men: Consider dark navy and gray suits. Wear pressed or starched shirts not taken directly from the dryer. White shirts are white, not yellowish. Ties are conservative.

Women: Wear colors that flatter. Avoid wearing multiple pieces of jewelry, especially dangling, chunky sorts. Wear clothing and accessories that make you look polished and professional. Make sure skirts are at least knee length. Wear hose and shoes with modest heels. Shoes have closed toes and backs. Err on the conservative side.

Code: Business Casual

Men: Avoid Khaki pants and "loud print" shirts. Consider dark-colored slacks with an Oxford shirt with muted colors and a conservative matching tie. If the weather is cold, pull on a solid color sweater. Another option is to wear dark slacks, solid or bold-line shirt, and a dark-colored sports coat or blazer. Belt and shoes should match.

Women: Consider wearing business skirts with appropriate blouses, such as silks, wool, or rayon with attractive prints. Nice slacks with a blazer or pants suits are also acceptable. Larger pieces of jewelry are acceptable for business casual. Flats or small heels are appropriate; wear hose and closed-toe (and back) shoes.

Code: Casual

Men: It is acceptable to wear khaki, navy or other basic-colored slacks. Polo-type shirts, "Camp" shirts or collared shirts long- or short-sleeved are appropriate. Stay away from blue jeans, denim, and sweat suit material. Shirts are to be crisp and colorful but not "neon-looking!" Avoid cut-off or jean shorts.

Women: Appropriate attire might be a skirt and blouse, or tailored slacks, blouse, and nice belt, attractive coordinated, flats, and hose. Avoid cut-off or jean shorts and body-conforming (distracting) clothing. Flip-flops and trendy open-toed or open-heeled shoes are taboo.

Source: http://business.missouri.edu/339/default.aspx

Resources: Dress for Success

John T. Molloy's New Dress for Success
by John T. Molloy. Publisher: Warner Books. ISBN #446385522.

New Women's Dress for Success
by John T. Molloy. Publisher: Warner Books. ISBN #0446672238.

Dress Casually for Success. . .For Men
by Mark Weber. Publisher: McGraw-Hill. ISBN #0070016224.

Esquire's Things a Man Should Know About Style
by Scott Omelianuk; Ted Allen. Publisher: Riverhead Books. ISBN #1573227633.

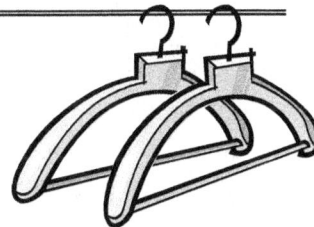

The Metrosexual Guide to Style: A Handbook for the Modern Man
by Michael Flocker.
Publisher: Da Capo Press.
ISBN #0306813432.

Make Mellow Mental Moments

When you feel yourself stressed and tense, try the following relaxation exercise. Take a 15-minute time-out. Make this time a scheduled appointment in your group calendar if you have to.

- Find a comfortable, quiet space in which to relax and recline (if possible).
- Take deep breaths – five-to-ten slow, full, deep breaths.
- Close your eyes.
- When you breathe in, silently say to yourself, "I am—"
- When you breathe out, silently say to yourself, "—relaxed."
- Feel your muscles gradually relax.
- Be aware of your body drifting lightly and feel a peacefulness come upon yourself.
- Continue breathing slowly, with your eyes closed.
- Allow your mind to drift to pleasant thoughts—or to nothing at all.
- At some point, begin to drift back to awareness of your surroundings.
- Slowly open your eyes to acclimate yourself to the here-and-now.
- Be conscious of feeling more relaxed, less stressed, and more at peace in the moment.

Resume normal activity more refreshed and energized. You will interpret people's comments and react to situations differently when you feel refreshed and energized from when you are tired and stressed.

Resources: Meditation and Relaxation Exercises

Instructions and audio downloads (MP3 files) for relaxation and meditation.
- Perform an Internet search on the terms "meditation and relaxation audio."
- Find a few favorites at SpringboardTraining.com/Programs/Just4U.

Positive Words

Why is it that you can say the same thing as your colleague, yet your colleague gets a positive response and you receive a less-positive one? It could be that the words you use reflect a less-than-positive expectation or outcome. Incorporate **positive words** into your messages when you communicate.

What are positive words? They are words that "feel" good, reflect a can-do expectation, and imply a belief that it is possible to achieve what is to be achieved. Examples of positive words include: can instead of cannot; do instead of do not; when will you instead of would you; we expect instead of we would like.

Use positive words in your letters, proposals, contracts, e-mail, and when you speak. They plant subliminal messages to the reader or listener that "no" is unacceptable and that you expect results. Positively!

Confident Comportment

Attitude is what makes a motorcycle rider a "biker." The clothes, swagger, posture, and way a biker looks at a non-rider communicates a confidence and strength that may or may not be the reality. The power presence creates the "bad biker" impression.

Your comportment influences how other people believe in and respect you. Use these communication techniques to project a confident image.

- Eliminate unnecessary filler-words from your speech. "Ummm", "sort of", "like", and "errrr" detract from your message. What detracts from your message makes your message weaker.
- Avoid butting. Make a positive statement, then use a "but" leading to a second statement and you invalidate the previous positive. Replace "but" with "and", or end with a period. Then move on to the next statement.
- End sentences with verbal periods. Your voice goes down at the end of a statement. When your voice goes up your statement becomes a question. Questions imply you need reassurance from the other person.
- Say what you mean. This is a cliché, yet we edit ourselves before we open our mouths. In business, ask direct questions and make the comments you want to make.
- Plan your points and know your desired outcome. Keep yourself on track by returning to your key points. Draw your communications to a close by focusing on your desired outcome.

People tend to follow, believe, and respect people who seem like they know what they are doing or saying. Communicate so that you seem like you do.

Syndicated column. © Sylvia Henderson. All rights reserved.

"If you have no confidence in <u>self</u>, you are twice defeated in the race of life. With confidence, you win even before you start."
– Marcus Garvey

"I have learned that success lies not in the destination, but in how you choose to take your journey. Success is living with integrity—in relentless pursuit of whatever it is that you are truly passionate about. What does this mean? It means that if you have spent every moment of your life striving to realize your absolute full potential in every way possible, then, and only then, can you consider yourself a success. Don't ever shy away from this success for fear of stepping outside your comfort zone or challenging the norm."
– Shaanah Valdez (Source: MotivateUs.com)

Pathways Scenarios: Set 1

Use for the activity at "Your Four Pathways to Positioning," p.14.

(1)

Ralph. Finance Department.

Ralph, one of three Finance Department employees, has been at his company for six years. He believes he is ready for the Finance Manager position and intends to speak up about it when the current manager retires in four months. Ralph is punctual, great with numbers, consistently turns in his reports accurately, and is known to help other employees figure out the company's complicated expense forms. He attended a few continuing education classes on corporate finance and has a few ideas he wants to implement once he is the department manager. He holds his ideas close to himself for now, lest another of his peers—with whom he has only cursory "as necessary' contact—steals his ideas. Since most of his day is spent at his cubicle, Ralph tends to hold personal grooming and professional attire as less significant to his job than his technical ability. In his current job, Ralph's interactions are with internal corporate personnel rather than external clients.

Address Ralph's positioning for becoming Finance Manager.

(2)

Serina. Federal Agent.

Serina is a mid-level Federal Agent in the Intelligence community. She loves what she does and has no desire to move into managing others. She presents an impeccable image and authoritative presence. Her "close rate" on solving cases is stellar. She hates paperwork and therefore, her reports and bulletins on procedural updates (suggested reading materials for keeping current with new methods) are piled in stacks on her desk. Physical fitness is important to her as well as is her volunteer work and social relationships. Therefore, when it is time to leave, she is adamant about leaving work behind. One month ago a new Bureau Chief began his position. His mandate is to trim his new budget and he is considering a reduction in the number of agents at particular levels as part of the process.

Address Serina's positioning as secure for job longevity.

(3)

Leslie. Recent Graduate; Entry-Level Employee.

Leslie has been on the job for seven months in an entry-level position. He is a "poster boy" for the EverReady™ battery bunny; he keeps going and going. He volunteers to tackle every challenge that presents itself. When he runs into problems with one task, he finds a way to delegate the remainder to someone else so he can move on to the next interesting challenge. His social network online (on the Internet) has hundreds of "friends" (contacts; connections) and he can usually be found communicating with them when not visibly or obviously (to his co-workers) working on his projects. His social skills person-to-person can stand improvement and his writing skills are poor, but he loves to give presentations and is great at managing the technology that goes with them. He vents his impatience with the seemingly slow pace of greater responsibility to anyone who will listen, and feels he should have a leadership position and higher pay than he currently has. He is uninspired in his current position and wants more flexibility.

Address Leslie's positioning for gaining more responsibility and challenge in the near future.

Pathways Scenarios: "Success Language" Cards

Card # Topic: Message:	Why does this message resonate with you?
What / which pathway(s) are represented by the message?	
Identify a related situation that most reflects your workplace / business / organization / life.	
What does the message mean to you for positioning for success?	

Humor—Lightness @ Work and in Life

You do not have to spend your life laughing, but it is good to laugh at life sometimes. Take life too seriously and you create physical stress for yourself. Life will happen whether you take it seriously or less so. You can remain focused on your goals and treat serious things seriously. In fact, you can be better at focusing and coping with the serious aspects of life if you find ways to counter seriousness with levity.

Take this self-assessment to determine your level of levity towards life.

Instructions: Rate yourself on a scale of 1-to-5, with 5 = "Describes me almost always" and 1 = "Describes me hardly ever."	1	2	3	4	5
1. I laugh out loud quite often and enjoy funny things.					
2. I appreciate irony and odd quirks in life.					
3. I look for the humor in serious situations.					
4. Others consider me as having a sense of humor and not taking life too seriously.					
5. I enjoy an occasional joke or cartoon.					
6. I laugh at my own mistakes and do not mind having fun poked at me appropriately.					
7. I use humor to quickly overcome a transgression against me.					
8. People find it difficult to stay mad at me because I have a light-hearted personality.					
9. My smile is genuine and my eyes light up and sparkle with wonderment.					
10. I sometimes act silly or do unexpected, outrageous things.					

Scoring: Total the numbers on the scale that correspond to each of your answers.   Total: [   ]

51-55:	You cannot add! Try again.
41-50:	You maintain a good sense of humor in your life.
25-40:	Consider applying techniques that allow yourself to lighten-up in life.
Below 25:	Seek help with learning to adjust your attitude to life before you experience the physical effects of stress.

Resource: Humor and Health

http://www.Jest4Success.com. Rosalind Trieber MS, CHES, CHP, NFL

> "Being happy doesn't mean everything is perfect. It means you have decided to look beyond the imperfections."
> – Unknown

More Attitude–Behavior Theory: The Betari Box

The Betari Box (also referred to as Betari's Box or Betaris Box) is a circular diagram that shows how attitude and behavior are linked.

Attitude affects behavior.

Our attitudes come out through our external behavioral displays. They may appear in the signals we send to other people (Ex: smiles, voice tone and use of particular words). They also appear in how we act, especially towards other people.

The same is true for others. The attitudes of other people affect their own behaviors.

Behavior affects others' attitudes.

When I do something or send physical signals to you, then it has an effect on your attitude. If I act in an aggressive way towards you, you interpret this in a certain way. Your attitude is affected by this, either because you are persuaded by my arguments or because you react to what you may perceive as unreasonable behavior by me.

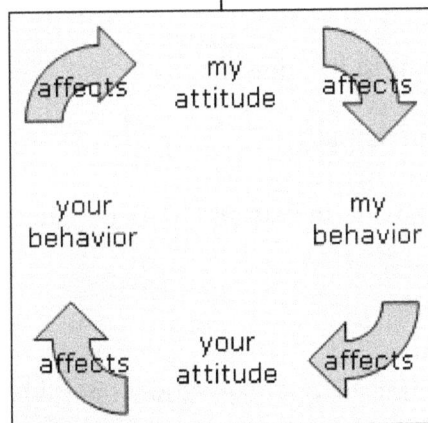

Again, the reverse is true. Your behavior affects my attitudes as I interpret, rightly or wrongly, what you do or signal. Thus, a circle is created. I act, which affects your attitude, which affects your behavior, which affects my attitude, which affects my actions. (See diagram below.)

So what?

This is a circular behavioral pattern where we get stuck in subconscious loops. Recognizing it is the first step to addressing it. To change the behavior of others, first examine your own attitude and how it affects your behavior. Then notice how your behavior affects other people. You can break the loop by noticing how the behavior of others makes you feel. Refuse to let it affect your attitude without first censoring this process.

Resources: Positive Attitudes / Authentic Living

- www.**selfgrowth**.com → articles, assessments, and resources for personal and professional development. (*Search for 'Sylvia Henderson' for published articles*).
- www.**motivation-tools**.com → articles, posters, references on motivation and success.
- www.**selfhelpmagazine**.com → articles, forums & discussion groups, resources, postcards. Psychology professionals.
- www.**personal-development**.com/chuck/index.html → hundreds (really!) of articles by self-development specialists.
- www.**powerofmyway**.com → a division of Dare Dreamers, LLC, whose purpose is to inspire and motivate you to live your life with authenticity, passion, and purpose.

"We are all serving a life sentence, and good behavior is our only hope for a pardon."
– Doug Horton

I Wish I Had That In School!

Springboard Training conducted a survey on LinkedIn to determine what knowledge and skills people, experienced in the workplace and in their professional endeavors, wish they had acquired "back in their school days". The actual survey query was:

> Name a skill that you use on the job, that you really wish you had learned while you were still in school. This skill most likely is something for which you would not have needed a whole separate course. But only you can tell for sure. Would this be important for those following after you to learn as well?

Here are a few of the most-repeated responses. All answered that those in school now will do well to learn these skills.

- How to write proposals. (Writing skills, plus more.) — (R.G.) Internet Strategist Media Solutions, Inc.
- Public speaking. Articulation of language. — (D.M.) DJ at Wireman.com
- Negotiating skills. — (E.L.) Non-Profit Executive
- Interpersonal skills. Learning how to understand other people. — (S.P.) Educator, Consultant, Author
- Conflict management. — (A.N.) Staffing Manager Homeless World Cup
- Sales and presentation skills. — (J.C.) Search Engine Marketer
- Political awareness and skills. (Office & organizational politics.) — (D.H.) Financial Expert
- Application of concepts learned in school: How to connect the theoretical concepts to the real world and the significance of what you learn at the school. — (M.S.) HW-SW Product Developer
- Ethics and integrity. How to take criticism. How to be professional. How to remain ethical even in the worst situations. — (G.T.) Freelance Consultant & Technical Writer
- Leadership skills…the "everyday leadership" skills non-managers need to practice. — (J.B., Ed.D.) Author and E-Learning Coordinator
- Personal financial management. (Balancing checking accounts, saving money, creating personal budgets.) — (J.C.) General Manager Web Industries
- Not making assumptions. — (J.M.) Non-Profit Executive
- How to make better use of my time. And reading for comprehension. — (T.B.) President Biggs Works, LLC
- Anger management. — (M.M.) Senior Copywriter MARC, USA
- How to handle stress; the "small stuff". — (L.J.) Motivational Speaker/Trainer/Recruiter
- That I don't have to do all the work for myself, by myself. — (R.B., Jr.) RODMON & Associates, Inc.

> "The most important function of education at any level is to develop the personality of an individual and the significance of [his] life to [himself] and to others. This is the basic architecture of a life. The rest is ornamentation and decoration of the structure."
> – *Grayson Kirk*

Life Events Scale: An Assessment of the Effects of Change in Your Life

(Based on the works of mental health experts Thomas H. Holmes and Richard H. Rache, *Holmes-Rahe Social Readjustment Rating Scale*. Journal of Psychosomatic Research.)

This stress assessment helps you identify the sources and amount of stress you encounter in your life. It was designed to predict the likelihood of disease and illness following exposure to stressful life events. Each life event is given a score that indicates the amount of readjustment a person has to make as a result of the event. Not all of the events in the scale are necessarily negative events.

This scale indicates that change in one's life requires an effort to adapt and then an effort to regain stability. Stress and feelings of loss are natural by-products of adapting and trying to regain a level "normalcy." This assessment considers only the events that occurred, not individual perceptions of the events in life. Perception is a key part of the total grief and loss experience, so while the Life Events Scale has value in increasing awareness of potential losses and life-changing or stressful events, an individual's perception of the event is an important variable to consider when assessing your overall health. For a more complete picture of how change affects your life consider all the dimensions of health: physical, mental, emotional, spiritual, and social.

Instructions

The following is a list of stress-inducing events in descending order of their Life Change Units. For each event that occurred in your life within the past year (prior 12 months, up to today), record the corresponding score. If an event occurred more than once, multiply the score for that event by the number of times the event occurred and record that score. The events refer to your life changes unless otherwise stated. Identify by the event itself (as it happened to you), regardless of whether you perceived it as positive or negative. NOTE: "Spouse" = life partner (long-term commitment; monogamous, regardless of legal stature).

Life Events (For Adults)	Life Change Units	My Score
Death of a spouse / life partner	100	
Divorce	73	
Marital separation	65	
Imprisonment	63	
Death of a close family member	63	
Personal injury or illness	53	
Marriage	50	
Dismissal from work	47	
Marital reconciliation	45	
Retirement (your own)	45	
Change in health of family member	44	
Pregnancy	40	
Sexual difficulties	39	
Gain a new family member (in whatever manner)	39	
Business readjustment	39	
Change in financial state	38	
Change in frequency of arguments	35	

Life Events (For Adults)	Life Change Units	My Score
Major mortgage acquisition	32	
Foreclosure of mortgage or loan	30	
Change in responsibilities at work	29	
Child leaving home	29	
Trouble with in-laws	29	
Outstanding personal achievement	28	
Spouse starts or stops work	26	
Begin or end school (you or your children)	26	
Change in living conditions	25	
Revision of personal habits	24	
Trouble with boss	23	
Change in working hours or conditions	20	
Change in residence	20	
Change in schools	20	
Change in recreation	19	
Change in church activities	19	
Change in social activities	18	
Minor mortgage or loan	17	
Change in sleeping habits	16	
Change in number of family reunions	15	
Change in eating habits	15	
Vacation	13	
Christmas (or equivalent significant holiday) alone	12	
Minor violation of law	11	
	My Total Score:	

Sylvia's note: This tool was developed prior to the use of cell phones and other portable electronic devices. Therefore, "loss of portable device or data" is not one of the significant life changes identified in the assessment. (This is meant to be a humorous statement…partially.)

Total your scores and see what they mean to your stress levels and their effect on your health.

Score of 300 +:   Warning…you have a high stress level. Your chance of accident or illness related to your stress during the next two years is great. Stress intervention techniques are strongly urged.

Score of 150-299 +:   Risk of illness is moderate (reduced by 30% from the above risk). Take care of yourself now. You have borderline high stress. Your chance of accident or illness related to your stress within two years is moderate.

Score <150:   Congratulations! At the moment, your stress level is low. Your chance of illness or accident related to your stress within two years is low. Remember that change—any change—can lead to additional stress, even enjoyable activities such as vacations or new forms of recreation.

Note: As of this printing, an online version of this assessment is available at http://health.discovery.com/centers/stress/balancing/stress/assessment_print.html.

What is "Murphy's Law"?

Murphy's Law ("If anything can go wrong, it will") is reputed to have originated at Edwards Air Force Base in 1949. It was named after an engineer, Capt. Edward A. Murphy. One day after finding an error on a project, Murphy cursed the responsible technician saying, "If there is any way to do it wrong, he'll find it." A project manager kept a list of "laws" and added Murphy's statement, which he called Murphy's Law. At a project press conference, the project safety record—which was good—was attributed to a firm belief in Murphy's Law and in the necessity to try and circumvent it. Aerospace manufacturers picked up the saying and used it widely in the ensuing months. Picked up and quoted in news and magazine articles, through repetitive media use Murphy's Law was born.

Source: http://www.murphys-laws.com

Who is Aesop and What Are "Aesop's Fables"?

A fable is a very short story. It tells us how to behave or teaches us a lesson. Frequently, fables are stories about animals that talk like people.

The lesson that a fable teaches us is called a moral. The morals are clearly stated in Aesop's fables.

Aesop is believed to have been a Greek slave who made up these stories to make his life easier. No one is really sure if Aesop actually existed, or, if he made up the fables attributed to him. What is certain, however, is that the stories called Aesop's Fables are so powerful and relevant that they have been told over and over again for thousands of years.

Many common sayings come from Aesop's Fables:
- "Don't count your chickens before they hatch."
- "Honesty is the best policy."
- "Look before you leap."

are familiar examples.

Whether a Greek slave named Aesop made up these stories, or many people living at different times made up the stories is not important. What is important is that the stories have survived and are worth re-telling because the morals are timeless.

A complete text of Aesop's fables is located at http://etext.lib.virginia.edu/toc/modeng/public/AesFabl.html.

"Individual commitment to a group effort -- that is what makes a team work, a company work, a society work, a civilization work."
– *Vince Lombardi*

"In any moment of decision the best thing you can do is the right thing, the next best thing is the wrong thing, and the worst thing you can do is nothing."
– *Attributed to Theodore Roosevelt, USA President #26*

Resources: Bibliography of Success Language Resources

Oxford Dictionary of English Grammar (Oxford Paperback Reference S.)
by Sylvia Chalker, E. S. C. Weiner. Publisher: Oxford University Press. ISBN #0192800876.

Merriam-Webster's Collegiate Dictionary
by Merriam-Webster. Publisher: Merriam-Webster. ISBN #0877798087.

The Oxford American Writer's Thesaurus
by Christine A. Lindberg, David Auburn, Michael Dirda (Editor), David Lehman (Editor), Stephin Merritt (Editor), Francine Prose (Editor), Zadie Smith (Editor), Jean Strouse (Editor), David Foster Wallace (Editor), Simon Winchester (Editor). Publisher: Oxford University Press.
ISBN #0195170768.

Webster's New World(tm) Dictionary and Thesaurus
by Charlton Laird, The Editors of Webster's New World. Publisher: Webster's New World.
ISBN #0764565451.

The Chicago Manual of Style
by University of Chicago Press Staff. Publisher: University Of Chicago Press. ISBN #0226104036.

The Elements of Style, Fourth Edition
by William Strunk Jr., E.B. White, Roger Angell. Publisher: Longman. ISBN #020530902X.

Words and Ideas: A Handbook for College Writing
by Hans Paul Guth. Publisher: Wadsworth Publishing Company. ISBN #0534008151.

Readers' Digest Magazine: *Word Power* column (word definitions and usage; monthly).

Internet Resources
- www.Dictionary.com (dictionary, word search, thesaurus, language forums) + http://dictionary.reference.com/wordoftheday/ (word-of-the-day)
- www.LibrarySpot.com (encyclopedias, Library of Congress, grammar lists, library links)
- www.m-w.com/dictionary.htm → Miriam Webster online (dictionary, thesaurus, encyclopedia, word-of-the-day, word games)
- www.WinstonChurchill.com (A Study In Oratory, from the Churchill Center)
- www.bartleby.com (Bartlett's Familiar Quotations)
- www.americanrhetoric.com/ (The power of oratory in the USA – speeches)
- www.historychannel.com/broadband/ (Speeches; need high-speed Internet connection)

Power Networking: Communication Skills for Technical Professionals
Author: Kate Zabrinski. ISBN #978-1935425076. www.BusinessTrainingWorks.com.

Communication Styles: A Self-Assessment
(Source: American Management Association)

Our accomplishments in the workplace often depend on how well we can communicate our needs and objectives to others. Truly effective communication requires an understanding of our own style as well as that of other people.

This short assessment gives you a foundation for discussion and for quickly determining how to best communicate with someone whose dominant communication style differs from yours.

Instructions:

Read each phrase and check the word across the corresponding row that <u>best describes</u> you. Then count up the check marks in each of the four columns and consult the Scoring Key to determine your dominant communication style.

	I	II	III	IV
1. Manner is basically	☐ accepting	☐ friendly	☐ controlling	☐ evaluative
2. Decision making	☐ slow	☐ emotional	☐ impulsive	☐ fact-based
3. I talk about	☐ personal things	☐ people	☐ achievements	☐ organization
4. Using time	☐ not rushed	☐ socializer	☐ rushed	☐ run late
5. Relate to others	☐ accepting	☐ empathizer	☐ commands	☐ assessing
6. Gestures	☐ sparse	☐ open	☐ impatient	☐ closed
7. Clothing	☐ conforms	☐ very stylish	☐ formal	☐ conservative
8. Work pace	☐ steady	☐ enthusiastic	☐ fast	☐ controlled
9. Listening	☐ interested	☐ distracted	☐ impatient	☐ selective
10. Work area has	☐ keepsakes	☐ pictures	☐ awards	☐ charts
11. Oriented toward	☐ support	☐ people	☐ results	☐ facts
12. Basic personality	☐ easygoing	☐ outgoing	☐ dominating	☐ no-nonsense
13. Communication	☐ low-key	☐ animated	☐ direct	☐ reserved
14. Responsiveness to others	☐ steady	☐ friendly	☐ restless	☐ distant
TOTALS:	I	II	III	IV
	Listener	**Creative**	**Doer**	**Thinker**

Communication Styles: A Self-Assessment (Scoring Key)

A score of … in a column:
- 7 or more = Strong Preference
- 5-6 = Moderate Preference
- 0-2 = Low Preference

Characteristics of Each Communication Style

These characteristics are generalizations for a dominant communication style. Most of us communicate using more than one style.

I. *Characteristics* of **Listeners**	II. *Characteristics* of **Creatives**
<ul><li>People oriented</li><li>Believe there is more than one method to achieve the same results</li><li>Demand a voice in decisions that affect them</li><li>Place a high premium on relationships</li><li>Can be slow decision makers</li><li>Don't delegate well</li><li>Seek security; don't take risks</li></ul>*Conflict:* Mainly with Doers *Suggest:* Try to be more assertive. Focus less on relationships and more on tasks. Learn to make observations based on facts, not subjective judgments.	<ul><li>Enthusiastic, excitement driven</li><li>Like public speaking and attention</li><li>May be too talkative</li><li>Persuasive and optimistic</li><li>Creative</li><li>Good sense of humor</li><li>Can be impulsive, make snap decisions</li><li>Have problems following through with an idea</li></ul>*Conflict:* Mainly with Thinkers *Suggest:* Slow down. Try to be less "intense."
III. *Characteristics* of **Doers**	IV. *Characteristics* of **Thinkers**
<ul><li>Pragmatic</li><li>Assertive</li><li>Results oriented</li><li>Competitive</li><li>Competent</li><li>Very verbal</li><li>Excellent problem solver</li><li>Risk taker</li><li>Can be arrogant and domineering</li><li>Can be poor listener and impatient</li></ul>*Conflict:* Mainly with Listeners *Suggest:* Slow down. Count to ten before responding. Learn to listen more. Work at showing your feelings, being more interested in relationships and being more open.	<ul><li>Detail oriented</li><li>Can be slow decision makers</li><li>Like rules and predictability</li><li>Lowest risk taker</li><li>Analytical</li><li>Conservative</li><li>Can be rigid, overly serious and indecisive</li></ul>*Conflict:* Mainly with Creatives *Suggest:* Try to move faster, show less need for endless detail, be less rigid about following policies. Take more risks. Show more personal concern for others.

Resources: Time, Calendar, and Scheduling

Franklin-Covey
http://www.franklincovey.com/foryou/
2200 West Parkway Blvd., Salt Lake City, Utah 84119
- Time management & personal productivity systems.
- Products. Electronic. Hand-held organizers. Training. Coaching services.
- Free articles with productivity and success tips.

Small Business Association
http://www.sba.gov/managing/growth/makingtime.html
Article about making time for success in your own business.

Day-Timers, Inc.
One Day-Timer Plaza. Lehigh Valley, PA 18195-1551
http://www.daytimer.com
- Time management & personal productivity systems.
- Products. Electronic. Hand-held organizers. Training.
- Free articles with productivity and success tips.

DayRunner, Inc.
http://www.dayrunner.com/
- Time management & personal productivity systems.
- Products. Electronic. Hand-held organizers.
- Free articles with productivity tips.

For Students: How to Study
http://www.howtostudy.org/index.php
Articles and tools specific to students and study habits.

Tools for Hand-Held Organizers (PDAs and Smart Phones)
"There's an app for that!" Search for tools at your communications provider's website.

Taming The Time Monster: How To Stop Procrastinating, Start Planning, & Get More Done
Author: Kate Zabrinski. ISBN # 978-1935425083. http://www.BusinessTrainingWorks.com

> "Avoid saying you don't have enough time. You have the same number of hours per day that were given to Helen Keller, Louis Pasteur, Michaelangelo, Mother Teresea, Leonardo da Vinci, Thomas Jefferson, and Albert Einstein."
> - H. Jackson Brown, Jr.

> "Time is a fixed income and, as with any income, the real problem facing most of us is how to live successfully within our daily allotment."
> – Margaret B. Johnstone

> "Does anybody know what time it is?
> Does anybody really care... About time?"
> – Chicago

Resources: Teamwork and Working Well With Others

- **Teams Rock!**
  http://www.teamsrock.com/articles-overview.asp
- **Teamwork is an Individual Skill: Getting Your Work Done When Sharing Responsibility**
  Christopher Avery, Meri Aaron Walker, and Erin O'Toole. Publisher: Berrett-Koehler.
  ISBN #1576751554. How to share responsibility with others to get work done when you do not have authority over them (and they don't have authority over you).

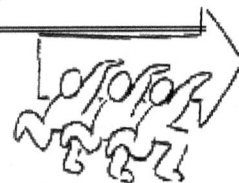

Time Management Tips

Interruptions:	• Schedule specific times (on your calendar) for e-mail; phone returns; visits; catch-up.
	• Make your rules clear; follow them (door closed; signal not to disturb; when to interrupt) – balance privacy with availability.
	• Use voice mail rather than constantly answering the phone when it rings.
	• Use key phrases to move people on (like, "Is there anything else?").
"Gate-keeper":	• Make clear who; when; under what conditions – allowed and "later".
Meetings:	• Schedule irregular times; just before meal or end-of-day.
	• Agenda; only those who need to attend; clear on purpose; start on time.
Organization:	• Schedule specific time on your schedule to organize; be ruthless.
	• Handle items one time through; a place for everything, or out the door.
	• Practice until process is part of you (becomes habit).
	• Respect yourself and others.
	• Create systems.
Efficiency:	• Multi-tasking vs. focus – some tasks require full attention; some can be performed simultaneously.
	• Work flow; travel flow.
	• Prioritize tasks; ask for deadlines.
	• Complete a task and then move on (avoid dallying / lingering).
	• Learn to say "no".
Procrastination:	• Commit to others; have accountability partners.
	• Set goals; reward self when goal milestones completed.
Balance:	• Over time → tend to physical, mental, emotional, spiritual health.
	• Put dates on the calendar; non-negotiable.
	• Schedule / take quiet time for yourself.
Where does it go?	• Document and analyze → get a handle on how you manage resources; be realistic.
	• Set goals; make changes accordingly.
	• Pay attention to details.
	• Make a list of the things you need to do the next day on the afternoon prior to leaving work.

"The strongest of all warriors are these two: time and patience."
– Leo Tolstoy

Teamwork: Mentoring Others

A new motorcycle rider learns the basic skills and safety procedures for riding in a motorcycle safety class. After earning a license, the new rider builds on the basics by riding with experienced riders. Experienced riders teach the advanced road, track, or trail skills that make newer riders successful riders.

When a new person joins your team in your professional field, one hopes they have the basic knowledge and skills needed to be a productive member of the team. By working with you and other experienced people, the new person gains the expertise and experience that helps them be successful team members and individuals. How can you be an effective mentor to another when you are busy with your own professional demands?

- Delegate some of your workload to a new person to free yourself and help them at the same time.
- Give specific instructions and be exact with deadlines and expectations.
- Establish checkpoints along the way where you evaluate specific, measurable results so as not to have surprises at the end.
- Give feedback using the sandwich approach. Tell something positive. Tell what can be improved or made more effective. Then end with something positive and encouraging.
- Suggest additional resources and study alternatives for further research and knowledge-building opportunities.

The more you help others succeed, the more successful you become.

Initiative—Be A "Leader of One"

On the highways and back roads you see both groups of motorcycle riders (two or more) and solo riders. In groups someone is always the leader – the first rider – in front. Solos are their own leaders – the front, middle, and rear rider all-in-one.

You are seldom alone as you travel through life. Rarely do you operate in a vacuum. When in a job where you work with other people, you may be a leader by nature of your profession or position. You take initiative, plan, instruct others, make things happen, and follow up. These are the basics of your responsibilities. At minimum, you are a leader of one…yourself.

Some ways to be a more effective leader of one include:

- Set goals for yourself and create the action plan–the interim steps you must take–to achieve your goals within a set timeframe.
- Write affirmations that are visions of what "success" looks, feels, sounds, tastes, and smells like to you. Say your affirmations out loud to yourself every day.
- Create a system that helps you organize– and keep organized–your time, communications, files, and resources all together. Implement your organization scheme and share it with others so that you discipline yourself to stick with it.
- Take time for yourself away from your regular demands. Stop what you are doing and walk away from it–for a few minutes, hours, or days, if you are lucky.
- Remember your priorities, and business should not be number one in your life. Even as an independent business person. Something or someone else should be most important to you in life.

When you steer yourself to your own destination, you are a leader of one.

Is It Work When There's Humor?

Humor has a direct impact on the way that work is done, thus having a direct impact on organizational success.

Humor makes business more <u>human</u>, processes more enjoyable and increases the likelihood that employees will work cooperatively towards meeting the organization's goals. In school, when teachers and professors do things differently— sometimes outrageously—by using some aspect of fun and humor in their classes, they make the process of learning more fun. If the process is more fun, students are more interested in participating. Learning outcomes are more successful as evidenced by research showing that students retain and recall information better when it is presented with humor.

The same principle applies to the work environment. If the work experience is more enjoyable, employees want to be there. They are more likely to contribute in a positive way. Humor improves the work environment by:

- Making communication easier and more effective. Humor and laughter reduce tension and enhance relationships.
- Causing a message to be more memorable. Humor helps you to convey information more effectively.
- Forcing us to see things differently. Humor is creativity packaged differently.
- Making us human. If we can laugh at our daily foibles, we can escape the grip of our egos and become more relatable.
- Making the mundane processes of our work more enjoyable. Adding an element of fun to meetings, projects and celebrations creates an environment in which people want to work.

Bottom line is, you may not make a million dollars by sharing a joke with your colleague. However, if you are willing to make the work environment more fun, you are worth your weight in gold!

Source: Ron Culberson, MSW, CSP. FUNsulting.com

Social and Professional Protocol: Telephone Etiquette

The following tips help you act and sound professional when you use a telephone as your communications tool. They pertain to both land-line and mobile telephone use.

- When you take a call, turn away from your computer, desk, and other distractions. Your attention should be on the caller.
- Have something available with which to write.
- Answer calls by the second or third ring.
- Smile when you answer your calls. Even though the caller cannot see it, they can hear the smile in your voice.
- Use a "telephone voice" in which you control your vocal volume and speed.
- Speak clearly.
- Be enthusiastic and respectful.
- Greet the caller and identify yourself and your business or organization (if applicable).
- Ask the caller, "To whom am I speaking?"
- Ask the caller, "How may I help you?"
- Avoid unnecessary jargon and acronyms.
- Use the caller's name in your conversation.
- Practice good listening skills.
- If there is a problem, be concerned, empathetic, and apologetic (if appropriate).
- Thank the caller for calling. Ask them to call again.
- Avoid eating, drinking, or chewing gum while you are on a call.

Source: Administrative Assistant's and Secretary's Handbook, by James Stroman, Kevin Wilson and Jennifer Wauson. Publisher: AMACOM. ISBN # 0814407846.

Social and Professional Protocol: E-Mail

- **Use formal "business" English** (in the USA). Avoid slang and jargon. Instant messaging, cell phone text messaging, and e-mail casual language, abbreviations, and emoticons are inappropriate in a business setting.

  Definition: emoticon – A typewritten picture of a facial expression, used in e-mail and when communicating on the Internet, to indicate emotion. Example: :-) as a happy face.

- **Grab the potential reader's attention** through the "Subject" line using a similar technique as news headlines. People are discriminating as to which e-mail they will open and read and which they will delete without opening in this age of spam, security issues, and lack of time.

  Definition: spam/spamming – The electronic equivalent of junk mail. The practice of sending copies of a message to many different recipients, with no regard to whether the subject matter is appropriate; or sending the same message by email to large numbers of people indiscriminately.

- Try to **limit the entire note to one screen** to minimize the reader's having to scroll down the screen. This takes practice and a lot of editing.

- **Avoid revealing "Send To" e-mail addresses** in notes that go out to multiple people. Use blind copies and blind distribution lists. (Your e-mail provider should have a "help" capability to tell you how to do this.)

- **Avoid forwarding e-mail** that you receive to other people. Highlight the e-mail text you want others to read, "copy" what you highlighted, then "paste" what you copied into a new e-mail addressed specifically to your target readers. This avoids forwarding potentially embarrassing or personal information as well as removes several lines of addressing and transmission identification that junks-up forwarded notes.

- Be diligent about staying up-to-date with e-mail addresses in **distribution lists**. Distribution lists become outdated in a matter of weeks due to individuals changing or dropping Internet Service Providers (ISPs), ISPs going out of business or changing business models, people changing their jobs, and any number of other factors. Most likely you will not be told of the changes so this is a proactive and regularly-scheduled   task.

"You can't talk your way out of a situation you behave yourself into."
– *Dr. Stephen Covey*

Written Communications: Perhaps You Might Reconsider

- "Kids Make Nutritious Snacks"
- "President Wins Budget. More Lies Ahead"
- "Stolen Painting Found by Tree"
- "Failed Panda Mating. Veterinarian Takes Over"

Social and Professional Protocol: Communicating in Writing

For formal letters and business writing, two "must-have" references are:
- The Chicago Manual of Style. University of Chicago Press. ISBN #0226104036.
- The Gregg Reference Manual. McGraw-Hill/Irwin. ISBN #0072936037.

Both are available at major bookstores, college bookstores, and online.

- Organize your thoughts and jot them down the first time without judgment / censorship. Then, rearrange what you note this first time to organize the information so that you make necessary connections between topics. Write a first draft of these notes.
  - Put the first draft aside for awhile and return to it with a fresh mind. Review the first draft and write a second draft—which will be a draft of the final product.
  - Have the second draft reviewed by other people and perform thorough edits.
  - The edited and corrected product from the review should be your final version that goes to the reader.

- Use "business" English (in the USA). Business English is conversational, yet direct and correct. It is seldom formal and legalistic.

- Avoid slang and jargon.

- Define terms and acronyms the first time you use them in each document—especially those unique to your industry or business environment.

- Use short sentences. Make your writing plain and clear. Avoid long words and complex sentences.

- Write in the present tense.

- Assume the reader has little time to read what you write. Be succinct. Get to the point within the first one-to-two sentences.

- Grab the reader's attention immediately through a question, challenge, "teaser" statement, or statistics.

- Take a cue from newspapers and magazines. Note how they grab your attention through their headlines, introduce the main points of interest and what you expect of the reader right away in the first paragraphs, then provide the supporting arguments and additional information in descending order of importance or impact. Use these techniques. Summarize everything and "close the sale" (call the reader to action).

- Use graphics where applicable. 21st Century messages are visually intensive (colorful, crowded, busy). Turn statistics into tables and charts. *USA Today*, *Time* and *Newsweek* magazines, and all-news satellite and cable channels are very effective at this. Study their techniques regardless of your personal politics.

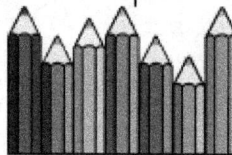

Write On! Tongue-in-Cheek Guidelines for Written Communications

- Verbs HAS to agree with their subjects. And don't start a sentence with a conjunction.
- Be more or less specific. Also too, never, ever use repetitive redundancies.
- No sentence fragments. One should NEVER generalize.
- Eschew ampersands & abbreviations, etc.
- The passive voice is to be ignored.
- Never use a big word when a diminutive one will suffice.
- Exaggeration is a billion times worse than understatement.
- Proofread carefully to see if you left any words out of your

Meetings

Meetings are a fact of life in any environment where two or more people are involved in getting something done. You might as well see to it that your meetings are as effective as they can be.

If *you are in charge* of the meeting:

- Ask yourself if the meeting is really necessary. Do you need a face-to-face meeting? Would a better alternative be a phone call, e-mail, or video conference?
- Invite as few people as possible. Only have the necessary participants attend.
- Have a written agenda with clear objectives. Make sure the agenda is circulated far enough in advance so that those who will attend can review the agenda and prepare for the meeting. Note time frames assigned for each item in the agenda.
- Be timely. Start and finish the meeting on time (or earlier). Respect your and everyone else's time.
- Select someone other than you to serve as the scribe. At the beginning of the meeting either ask for a volunteer or select a trusted participant.

This person monitors the timing and takes appropriate notes. You have to concentrate on fulfilling the purpose of the meeting.

- If the meeting is longer than one hour – which you should avoid as much as possible – allow everyone a stand-up-and-stretch break without leaving the room.
- Ask everyone to turn off phones and other devices. People have been known to survive without their devices for an hour and live to tell about it afterwards!
- Circulate the meeting minutes and action items within 2-to-3 days of the meeting. Make sure the action items have responsible people and "by when" dates noted for each.
- And finally … avoid calling meetings unless you absolutely must.

Even if *you are not in charge* of the meeting:

- Prior to the meeting, ask the person calling the meeting what they hope to accomplish, who is invited, how long the meeting will be, and what specific information you need to bring with you.
- Request an agenda before the meeting.
- Vague answers may indicate a lack of preparation or solid thought about the meeting being called. Share your concerns with the person calling the meeting and offer suggestions to help ensure a better-run meeting.
- Review materials in advance and come prepared.

- Decline the invitation to participate if you feel you are not needed or cannot contribute.
- Block the meeting times on your calendar. Allow for travel to and from the meeting in your time blocks.
- Ask the meeting chair to clarify objectives and confirm timing at the beginning of the meeting.
- Request that the meeting chair list the discussion items on paper if no agenda is offered.
- If the group seems unfocused throughout a discussion, ask for or give a brief summary of the key discussion points to refocus the group's attention. Remind everyone that

there are other agenda items to cover in the allotted timeframe.

- Suggest that a seemingly unresolvable issue be addressed in a different manner – a separate meeting, a special committee or task force, one person collecting more

information to present to the group at a later time, or simply delegating the issue to one or two people to resolve.

- Point out that additional issues not planned for the current meeting may best be handled at a different time.

Positive Work Environment: You Work the Controls

Stuff happens! Constantly. At work. In your volunteer duties. At play. In your family. Many aspects of the journey of "life happens" are beyond your control. However, you can control how you steer through your journey and you can be a ride leader for others. How you react to issues, and what you bring with you to your workplace, can have a very real effect on how people perceive you and whether you are considered to be a positive leader.

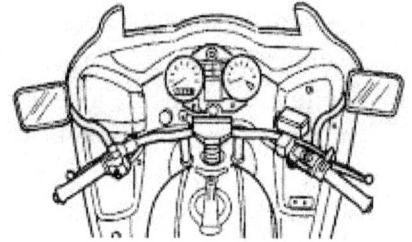

You can view "life happening" one of two ways: either as a victim, or as a leader who moves around or through the challenges. These are tips for being a proactive leader who works the controls and maneuvers through to positive outcomes. Suit up, and let's roll.

- Take charge of your personal life. Come to work ready to get your job done.
- Demonstrate your added value. Recognize that each decision, suggestion, action, and plan links to the long-term stability and growth of your organization.
- Have a positive impact. No one but you need know your inner attitudes, beliefs, and feelings. Your employer has the right, however, to evaluate how you behave and perform on paid work time as a result of your attitudes, beliefs, and feelings.
- Embrace and initiate change. Change is a permanent and necessary workplace fixture. Employers need people who are resilient and can face change without resorting to complaints, apathy, or anger.

- Work smarter, harder, and more efficiently. Know what needs to be done, and do it. Find ways to make things better for yourself and for your colleagues.
- Communicate openly and directly. Effectively express your ideas, preferences, and feelings to your colleagues, clients, and management. Open communications creates a trusting, respectful climate.
- Look for leadership opportunities. Volunteer to give presentations. Offer to help others. Good leaders are positive role models and build relationships that cause them to be viewed as trustworthy, resilient, positive, and visionary.

Source: Notes from "Creating a Positive Workplace When You're Not In Charge" seminar.

"Control your own destiny or someone else will."
– Jack Welch

Social and Professional Protocol: Let's Eat Out (Dining Etiquette)

Emily Post's Thumbed Index of Etiquette
Publisher: HarperResource.
ISBN: 0066209579.

Emily Post's The Guide to Good Manners for Kids
by Cindy Post Senning, Peggy Post, Steve Bjorkman.
Reading level: Ages 9-12.
Publisher: HarperCollins.
ISBN: 0060571969.

Miss Manners' Guide to Excruciatingly Correct Behavior
by Judith Martin, Gloria Kamen (Illustrator).
Publisher: W. W. Norton & Company.
ISBN: 0393058743.

Business Etiquette for Dummies
by Sue Fox.
Publisher: For Dummies.
ISBN: 0764552821.

Internet Resources
- www.everyrule.com/etiquette.html
- www.emilypost.com/etiquette/business
- business.missouri.edu/342/default.aspx
- www.washingtonpost.com →
  Miss Manners™ etiquette columns

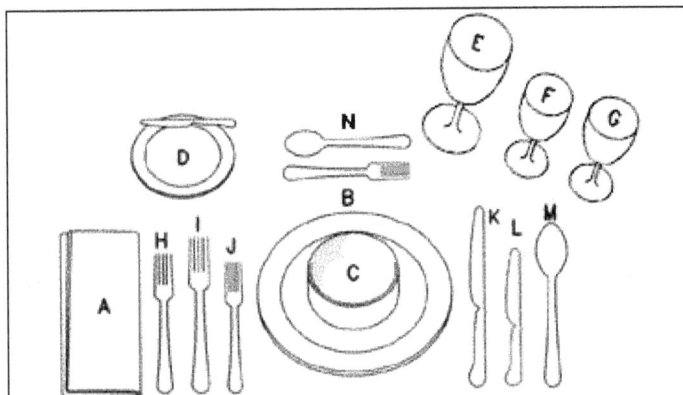

A	Serviette (napkin)
B	Service plate
C	Soup bowl on plate
D	Bread and butter plate with butter knife
E	Water glass
F	White wine
G	Red wine
H	Fish fork
I	Dinner Fork
J	Salad fork
K	Service knife
L	Fish knife
M	Soup spoon
N	Dessert spoon and cake fork

Note: Frequently, the salad fork (J) is placed to the left of the dinner fork (I). However, in this formal setting the dinner fork is placed to be used before the salad fork because it is suggested that the guest awaits the main meal before having salad.

(Source: www.didyouknow.cd/info/tablesettings.htm)

When YOU Are the Host : "It may look like lunch, but it's business!"

- When inviting a client to lunch, remember that the restaurant you select is subconsciously perceived as an extension of your office. Therefore, select a restaurant where the food is of good quality and the service is reliable.
- When escorted to a table by a maitre'd, allow your guest(s) to walk behind the person. When finding a table on your own, take the lead.

- Be sure to extend the "power" seat to your client. Seat yourself with your back facing the door/main body of the room.
- Once everyone is seated, place your napkin on your lap. This gesture serves as a cue that the meal is about to begin.
- When making a food recommendation, recognize that most guests also take your suggestion as the price range to stay within.

- When the server asks for your meal order before your guests', it's the perfect time to say, "I'd like my guest(s) to order first." Besides being appropriate, it's a cue to let the server know that the check should be left with you at the end of the meal.

- When reaching for the bread basket, salad dressing, etc., offer them to your guest(s) BEFORE using them yourself.
- Finally, tip adequately. Treat the server as one of your employees. It is a small price to pay for good service, personal attention, and the business that you land.

Source: http://business.missouri.edu/343/default.aspx

In Position for the Curves—Initiate <u>Your</u> Attitude Change

I learned to ride a motorcycle by taking a Motorcycle Safety class. In the class I learned that to handle curves in the road successfully, I must SLOW the vehicle before entering the curve, LOOK ahead through the curve to determine road conditions and curve sharpness, LEAN the motorcycle into the curve and position it at the widest point of the curve, and ROLL on the throttle (give the bike gas) to accelerate through the curve for the best tire traction. Over the years I realized that I apply the same process to my interactions with people.

Consider that our attitudes affect how we behave—what we do and how we react to external forces. Many of the external forces involve what other people say and do to, with, and around us. We allow other people's actions and words affect our attitudes. When our attitudes are negative, we act negatively. Our actions towards others cause them to act and react in kind. It's a viscous circle!

The Attitude—Behavior—Reaction loop identifies this circle. Note that I previously said that we <u>allow</u> other people to influence our attitudes. The realization that I allow this to happen causes me to also allow myself to check my attitude and respond differently. We can control how we react to people…in spite of how much and how long we endure the external stimuli that set our attitudes in the first place. We can end the negative attitude—behavior loops and create repeated loops of positive attitudes and behaviors. While we cannot "make each other" behave in certain

ways, we can influence each other by how we interact with each other.

Follow the process motorcyclists follow to handle curves in their roads in order to handle the curves of the attitude—behavior—reaction loops you experience in your life.

🏍SLOW.
Stop or ease-up on the assumptions you make as to why someone says or does what they do. Catch yourself before you immediately react to a slight or perceived wrong. Check your attitude. Consider that what someone else does, and the possible whys, are their issues. Ask yourself what you might have done or said to provoke their actions or encourage their words. Consider, also, that their issues may not be about you. You were just there at an opportune moment for them.

🏍LOOK.
Consider your alternatives for adopting a particular attitude. You have a choice. Think about the consequences and import of your actions and reactions. Give thought to the words you can, might, or will say. Decide to avoid falling into negative traps. You have the power to surprise someone with your pleasant attitude.

🏍LEAN.
Give conscious thought to laying your plan to keep—or change—your attitude for the positive. Set your course for how you will react. Contradict other people's

expectations if they expect you to react negatively.

🦽ROLL.

Follow through with positive behaviors. Carry out your plan to maintain a positive attitude. Do what you need to do to treat another person in the manner you wish to be treated. Be your attitude change.

Then experience the difference in another person's reaction to you.

While simplistic in its description, this process may take time—and multiple loops—to take effect for you. Be patient and keep practicing. I still consciously think through each curve in the road I encounter in my travels when I ride, many years after that Motorcycle Safety class. The difference is that, with practice and consistency, the process comes more naturally to me. I feel wonderful when I emerge from the curves. A similar effect results from emerging from the attitude—behavior—reaction loop with a positive attitude and positive behaviors. Get good at taking the curves!

The Travelers and the Monk

One day a traveler was walking along a road on his journey from one village to another. As he walked he noticed a monk tending the ground in the fields beside the road. The monk said "Good day" to the traveler, and the traveler nodded to the monk. The traveler then turned to the monk and said, "Excuse me, do you mind if I ask you a question?" "Not at all," replied the monk.

"I am traveling from the village in the mountains to the village in the valley and I was wondering if you knew what it is like in the village in the valley?" "Tell me," said the monk, "What was your experience of the village in the mountains?" "Dreadful," replied the traveler. "To be honest, I am glad to be away from there. I found the people most unwelcoming. When I first arrived I was greeted coldly. I was never made to feel part of the village no matter how hard I tried. The villagers keep to themselves. They don't seem to take kindly to strangers. So tell me, what can I expect in the village in the valley?"

"I am sorry to tell you," said the monk, "but I think your experience will be much the same in the valley." The traveler hung his head despondently and walked on.

A while later another traveler was journeying down the same road and he also came upon the monk. "I'm going to the village in the valley," said the second traveler. "Do you know what it is like?" "I do," replied the monk." But first tell me—from where have you come?"

"I've come from the village in the mountains." "And how was that?" "It was a wonderful experience. I would have stayed if I could but I am committed to travelling on. I felt as though I was a member of the family in the village. The elders gave me much advice, the children laughed and joked with me, and people were generally kind and generous. I am sad to leave from there. It will always hold special memories for me. And now, what of the village in the valley?" he asked again.

"I think you will find it much the same," replied the monk. "Good day to you". "Good day and thank you," the traveler replied. And he smiled, and journeyed on.

This page intentionally blank.

Pathways Scenarios: Set 2

Use for activity at "Attitude ➲ Behavior ➲ Reaction Loop," p.24.

GROUP A		Common Aspects / Characteristics
1		
2		
3		
4		
5		

	SLOW	LOOK	LEAN	ROLL
GROUP B				

Reference: "In Position for the Curves—Initiate Your Attitude Change," on p.92.

Pathways Scenarios: Set 3

Use for activity at "Get Along With 'Difficult People' In Difficult Situations – Manage and Mitigate Conflict," p.54.

	How do you handle this difficult situation?
Jonetta (your **boss**) and you attend meetings together. You can barely speak a few sentences before she interrupts you. She frequently adds her own comments or fills-in information that you are going to say in a few minutes. This is Jonetta's modus operandi; she does this on a regular basis. You observe other people's annoyance after this happens often enough.	**A**
A **co-worker** demands that you do part of his job and then does not give you credit for having done so. He barges into your open workspace uninvited and leans closely towards you when he speaks. You find his voice loud and ingratiating and his breath, unpleasant. When people see him coming around the corner they disperse and find other things they suddenly have to do. He seems to focus his attention on you the most for signs of weakness.	**B**
Two of **your customers (or clients)** consistently argue in front of you. They openly disagree with each other in meetings. One believes plans will not succeed as scheduled; the other believes things turn out for the best. At times, the two are verbal with their disagreements; at other times they ignore each other or rudely talk over each other. They use "lightly profane" language with each other, but never directly to you or anyone else. You, and everyone else you observe, feel uncomfortable during these displays. However, they are you customers / clients and you depend on them for a significant part of your business.	**C**
You ask **your Administrative Assistant**, who also supports a group of your colleagues, to handle tasks he should handle for you as part of his job description. He says he will take care of things, then routinely puts your requests on his back-burner in favor of another colleague of yours. When this other colleague and you are together, the AA focuses his attention on the other. You end up doing what you asked of him because you have deadlines to meet. Yet, he continues to accept your requests when you give him things to do.	**D**
Your own scenario?	

Solid Social Support Networks

Social interaction with family and friends who have positive outlooks on life is an integral element of mental and physical health.

We need contact, encouragement, support, love and interaction with others to be happy and well balanced. When we neglect social interaction, our health suffers. Social support and interaction affect:

- How well you cope with stress in life.
- How happy, content, depressed, or lonely you are.
- Your body's immune system.
- How well you survive when faced with crises or serious illness.
- Predictors of how long you live.

A study called the Good Health Practices study (Breslow and Belloc, Good Health Practices Study) observed 6500 people for over nine years. The study revealed that people with poor social support networks are two-to-three times more likely to die (2.3 times for men, 2.8 times for women) than those with strong social support systems. Social support and interaction have positive affects on both physical and mental health.

The indicators linked to a strong social network and longevity used in the study were:

- Being married (having a monogamous life-partner relationship).
- Having frequent contact with family and close friends.
- Being an active member of a faith-based institution.
- Actively participating in a club or other social group.

A six-year study of 17,000 healthy men and women revealed that people who are most isolated and lonely, with little social contact, are four times more likely to die within the same period of time as those with strong social contacts and support. Other studies show that people with strong social supports are more likely to survive after surgery or serious illness.

Strategies for Improvement

Consider these suggested strategies for improving your social health:

- *Invest in friendships.* Take time to meet new people, and renew old friendships. Stay in contact. Meet often and do things together. Positive social interaction enriches your social and emotional life.
- *Keep in close contact with those you consider your family (in a positive light).* Staying in touch, visiting, doing things together brings joy to your life and others.
- *Invest in a strong, life-long love relationship,* or develop a close confidant — one with whom you can share your most private fears and worries, your successes and joys, and with whom you can give and receive love.
- *Join a group.* Community, faith-based, and social organizations provide values-supportive ways to meet new people and develop caring friends.
- *Volunteer.* Many social organizations need volunteers. Volunteering is a way to stay involved and help other people while finding social outlets for yourself.
- *Look for social opportunities* (or create them) to do things with people. Invite people over or out to dinner. Watch a movie or do something mutually fun together. Take a class.

For optimal social and mental health, interact with positive people. People are more important than things. Time spent with positive people helps you enjoy a long and fulfilling life.

Compiled from multiple health and well-being sources.

Resources: Personal and Emotional Issues

You Choose! Dealing With Family and Personal Issues

You can choose [   ],

but you cannot choose [   ].

Challenge: Choose [   ].

Employers typically have their own resources to which you can turn for private, personal concerns. If, however, you need help that, for whatever reasons, you choose to seek outside of your workplace resources, the following organizations are good places with which to start. Each of these organizations can refer you to the resources you need for your unique situation.

Employee Assistance Professionals (EAP) Association
http://www.eapassn.org
(703) 387-1000

American Psychological Association
http://www.apa.org/
750 First Street, NE, Washington, DC 20002-4242
Telephone: 1-800-374-2721; (202) 336-5500
TDD/TTY: (202) 336-6123

National Association of Social Workers
http://www.naswdc.org/
750 First Street, NE, Suite 700, Washington, DC 20002-4241
NASW switchboard: (202) 408-8600

"Be daring, be different, be impractical, be anything that will assert integrity of purpose and imaginative vision against the play-it-safers, the creatures of the commonplace, the slaves of the ordinary."
- *Cecil Beaton*

Interpersonal Skills / Personal Image—Portable Skills That Position You for Success
Use for short program.

"Portable skills" = skills that transfer across professions, jobs, careers, and social involvements. They apply to the relationship-oriented aspects of your life.

◈ Grooming / attire.

◈ Personal presence – "Look of Success".

◈ Attitude – effect on behavior.

◈ Language skills – verbal and written communications.

◈ Body language / other non-verbal signals.

◈ Listening skills / synthesizing and making decisions.

◈ Messages you convey – positive and negative.

◈ Timeliness / managing time and priorities.

◈ Work ethic.

◈ Social and business etiquette / getting along together in the workplace.

◈ Busy vs. results – accomplishments / achievements / recognition.

◈

"The trick is in what one emphasizes. We either make ourselves miserable, or we make ourselves happy. The amount of work is the same."
— *Carlos Castaneda*

SPRINGBOARD
TRAINING

Springboard Training • www.springboardtraining.com • Sylvia@SpringboardTraining.com
P.O. Box 588, Olney, MD 20830-0588

Program Feedback and Evaluation Form

Program: "Pathways to Positioning"   Date: _____   Facilitator: _____

1 -------------------3-------------------- 5
Excellent   Average   Poor
○   ○   ○   ○   ○

Please rate the following aspects of the program:

		1	2	3	4	5	
1.	Content (topics)	○	○	○	○	○	Comments:
2.	Program Resource Manual©	○	○	○	○	○	Comments:
3.	Program appropriate to your needs (professional/personal)	○	○	○	○	○	Comments:
4.	Facilitator's classroom facilitation skills	○	○	○	○	○	Comments:
5.	Facilitator's knowledge of the content (topics)	○	○	○	○	○	Comments:
6.	Facilitator's organization and time management	○	○	○	○	○	Comments:

Other things I have to say about this program or facilitator…

I suggest you contact the following person about bringing more of your programs to our organization:

This page intentionally blank.

Resources: Personal & Professional Development, from Springboard Training

- www.SpringboardTraining.com
- www.Subscribe2Succeed.com

Pocket Reference Books© from Sylvia Henderson and Springboard Training:

- *Stuff for Busy People: Proven Techniques You Can Use for Being an Effective Communicator.*
- *Stuff for Busy People: Proven Techniques You Can Use to Communicate, Cope, and Lead in Uncertain Times.*
- *Tips for Busy People: Proven Techniques You Can Use to Present Powerful Presentations.*
- *Stuff for Busy People: Leadership Lessons for Life (for Leaders of All Levels)*
- *Stuff for Busy People: 52 Motivational Moments to Help You Succeed.* Compilation.
- *Stuff for Busy People: Pathways to Positioning—40 Proven Techniques You Can Use to Position Yourself for Success.*

Compact Disk✪ *Stuff for Busy People: Effective Communication – Critical Skills You Need to Succeed, in Less Thank One Hour.* Audio program, handout, article for newsletter, from Springboard Training.

Everything is available online at www.SpringboardTraining.com/Products/Invest-success.

Reasons to Celebrate!	
Time Management Month	February
Ideas Month	March
Effective Communications Month	June
Self-Improvement Month	September
Positive Attitude Month	October
No Interruptions Day	December *(Last biz day)*

Reference: Chase's Calendar of Events, or www.SpringboardTraining.com.

Card Deck: *Success Language* (Daily reminders, and activity tool, from this program…and more. Boxed set of 26 cards + case.)

Book: *Profetiquette (Professional Etiquette): What to Do and Say to Excel at Work and Pay.* Sylvia Henderson. V-Twin Press. ISBN # 9781932197303.

============================

Sylvia Henderson, Founder / CEO—Springboard Training: Bio

Sylvia Henderson **helps people show that they are as great as they say they are**. She facilitates **workshops and conference general sessions, keynotes, develops educational tools,** and authors **books and program-related articles**.

Sylvia integrates principles of adult learning into her programs by **actively engaging audiences in the learning process**, using training aids to generate interest and emphasize points. She weaves her avocation as a motorcyclist into analogies and metaphors that tie into messages targeting your needs.

Sylvia's **real-world experiences** include 30+ years as a corporate trainer, team leader and manager **practicing** the leadership, communication and motivational **skills she now presents in her programs**. She serves on several Boards of Directors and is Past-President of a national non-profit association and professional association local chapter.

Find articles, view videos, and listen to audio lessons from Sylvia and Springboard Training at SpringboardTraining.com. Receive continuous learning tools delivered to your door and online by subscribing as a member to Subscribe2Succeed.com. Bring Sylvia to your organization for additional training and to speak at your next event. Contact her at SpringboardTraining.com/contact.

SPRINGBOARD
TRAINING

www.ingramcontent.com/pod-product-compliance
Lightning Source LLC
Chambersburg PA
CBHW051226200326
41519CB00025B/7262